Take Control of Your Health

How to Quickly, Safely, and Affordably Master the Art of Wellness

Craig Brockie
foreword by Dr. Lorne Swetlikoff, ND

Ascension Int'l Group Inc.

Published by Ascension Int'l Group Inc.
369-1027 Davie Street
Vancouver
British Columbia
V6E 4L2
Canada

Copyright © Craig-Edward:Brockie 2009

All rights reserved. No part of this publication may be reproduced in any form or by any means without the prior permission of the publisher.

While every effort has been taken to ensure accuracy, the authors and the publisher make no representations about the accuracy of the information contained in this book and cannot accept responsibility for any errors or omissions, or for any loss based on the content of this book. Where links to websites have been included, these are offered as a resource for readers. No warranty is given about the information or products that may be available from any of these websites and no endorsement is made of any site listed in this book.

The information provided in this book is for information purposes only and is not intended as a substitute for advice from your physician or other health care professional. This book has not been evaluated by Health Canada or the United States Food and Drug Administration. This book does not diagnose, treat, cure, or prevent disease.

All trademarks are property of their respective owners.

Stick man image on cover © Elisanth | Dreamstime.com

ISBN: 978-0-9813693-0-3

Dedicated to all those who seek empowering knowledge and take action to improve their health and the lives of others.

Acknowledgements

I would like to thank:

My parents, Ruth and Ted Brockie, for being the best parents I could have asked for. You taught me to believe in myself, always tell the truth, treat everyone with respect, and the value of hard work. Thank you for always being there when I needed you.

My sister, Lisa, for her extraordinary example of being in service and her dedication to improving the health and lives of others.

My wife, Alina, for being the love of my life, my rock, and for being by my side throughout this incredible journey.

My sons, Skylar and Ronan, for bringing so much joy to my life, teaching me the importance of being present and not taking life too seriously.

Nigel Jeffers for getting me onto the right track. You are the real deal and a true gift to humanity.

Dr. Jan Chelowa and Dr. Lorne Swetlikoff for giving me back my immune system.

Dr. Dean Howell, Dr. Greg Blaney, Dr. Chad Alderson, and Jimmy Choi for eliminating my pain and optimizing my structure.

Dr. Sabina DeVita and Geoff Riley for teaching me

about EMF pollution and introducing me to the fascinating field of energy medicine.

Phil Naudi for getting me excited about ozone and for watching my back.

Ed McCabe, Dr. Ali Abdullah, Dr. Louie Yu, and Ross Anderson for your heroic work with oxidative therapies.

Shelina Manji, Juan Ruitz Naupari, David Raphael, Ross Kerr, and Cory Herter for keeping me clear, boosting my energy and expanding my world of possibilities.

Tibor Palatinus, Dr. Allan Sosin, Dr. Victoria Cupic, Henry Diaz, Christopher Smith, Skye Logan, and the rest of the team for giving me my father back.

Wayne Gretzky, Jack Canfield, Wayne Dyer, Bryan Tracy, Harvey McKay, Roger Dawson, Stephen Covey, and Tony Robbins for being great role models, motivating me to achieve, and/or teaching me what I needed to learn.

Buckminster Fuller, Kevin Trudeau, David Icke, Robert Prechter, Gary Renard, Michael Talbot, Bob Frissel, Richard Gerber, Adam Dreamhealer, Harry DeLigter, and Paul Verge for inspiring me to fearlessly share empowering knowledge.

All those who are chronically ill, living in pain, or have lost a loved one to an "incurable" disease for inspiring me to write this book.

About the Author

Craig Brockie has invested more than a decade and over a million dollars traveling the world and researching advanced health and performance enhancing technologies.

Craig was inspired to study wellness as a result of losing his health early in life, living most of his twenties with chronic pain, disease, and extreme levels of anxiety. After hitting the wall with what conventional medicine had to offer, he began exploring holistic medical solutions, learning that there was much more to them than the limited scope attributed to these ideas. With first-hand experience of a range of modalities guided by the best practitioners in their respective fields and successful results from many unique breakthrough treatments, Craig is now in a position to talk authoritatively about these treatments with a passion for sharing them with others.

Craig is a retired internet search engine marketer. Incredibly grateful for the abundance in his life, he now focuses his attention on humanitarian projects and private investing. He lives in a tranquil oceanfront setting near Vancouver, Canada with his wife and two sons.

Table of Contents

Foreword — **XIII**
Introduction — **1**
How Do You Feel About Your Health? — 1
My Story: Why Did I Get Interested In My Health? — 2
Pointing Fingers — 7
What Now? — 10
Winners Keep Score: Assessment — 13

Chapter 1
Rinse Yourself Out — **15**
Human Toxicity — 16
Toxic Build-Up — 17
Let's Get Moving! — 19
Now Rinse — 20
  Internal Body Wash Step 1: Ingredients — 21
  Internal Body Wash Step 2: Making the Broth — 21
  Internal Body Wash Step 3: Consuming the Broth — 22
  Internal Body Wash Step 4: The Rinse Cycle — 22
  Internal Body Wash Step 5: Repeat — 23
  Internal Body Wash: Reactions and Results — 23
  Internal Body Wash: Cycle Finished — 24
Chlorinated Water — 25
Integrating the Internal Body Wash into Your Daily Routine — 26
Now Your Colon's Clean... — 26

Chapter 2
How Are You Feeling? — **29**
The Effect of the Mind on Health — 30
  The Placebo Phenomenon — 30
  Personality Disorders — 30
Stress — 31
  Shallow Breathing — 31

Increased Blood Pressure and Erratic Heart Rate	32
Raging Hormones	32
Results of a Stressful Lifestyle	33
The Interrelation between Health and Stress	34
Addressing Emotion-Related Illness	35
Personal Counseling Therapy	36
Energetic Medicine	38
The Eastern Influence in Energetic Medicine	38
Emotional Freedom Techniques	40
Magnesium	41
Aromatherapy	41
The Raindrop Technique	43
Tantra	44
What Are You Believing?	44
Are We Healthy or Are We a Victim of Disease?	45
Do We Live in a Friendly, Abundant World or a Hostile World of Scarcity?	46
Are We Justified in Living Each Day In Fear?	47
Do We Truly Love Ourselves?	48
Applied Kinesiology	48
EFT, BodyTalk, and ThetaHealing	49
Fasting... from the News and External Distractions	50
Voltage	51
Supercharge Your Life with Sacred G	52
Enhancing Your Household Water Supply	53
Electromagnetic Field Pollution	54
Other Ways to Reduce Stress and Maximize Happiness	55
Naturopathic Medicine	55
Vibrational Remedies	55
Group Healing	56
Headphone Sessions	57
Do What You Love	58
Exercise	59
Be Happy Every Day	59
Now You've Improved How You Feel...	61

Chapter 3
Flood Your Body with Oxygen 63

Oxygen Starvation 65
Breathe Deeply 68
Oxygen Supplements 71
  Hydrogen Peroxide 72
  Stabilized Oxygen Supplements 75
  Topical Oxygen Supplements 76
Medical Oxygen Therapies 77
  Hyperbaric Oxygen Therapy 77
  Intravenous Hydrogen Peroxide 78
  Ozone Cupping, Bagging, and Steam Cabinets 79
  Ozone Insufflation 79
  Ozone Autohemotherapy 80
  Direct Intravenous Ozone Injection 82
  EBOO Ozone Treatments 83
  Other Ozone Therapies 84
Getting More Oxygen Every Day 85
  Violet Ray 85
  Oxygenated Water Cooler 85
  Improving Indoor Air Quality 86
Getting More Oxygen 87

Chapter 4
Acidosis: Putting Out the Fire 89

pH 90
pH and Oxygen 91
Acidosis 92
Reducing Acid in the Body 93
  Reduce Stress 94
  Breathe Deeply 94
  Alkaline Water 95
  Alkalizing Diet 96
  Minerals 97
  Bicarbonate 98
An Alkaline Life 99

Chapter 5
Taking Out the Trash: Bacteria, Virus, and Parasite Elimination — 101

Bag of Dirty Water — 102
  Clearing Toxins — 102
  Avoiding a Healing Crisis — 103
  Supporting the Immune System — 104
Taking Out the Trash — 105
  Viruses and Parasites — 105
  Candida — 106
  Bacteria — 108
  Antibiotics — 108
  Probiotics — 109
  Removing Candida — 110
Calling for Trash Collection — 112

Chapter 6
Healing from the Inside Out — 113

Understanding Enzymes — 114
Food Sensitivities — 116
Food Combining — 119
What Should I Eat? — 120
What Supplements Should I Take? — 121
  Minerals — 122
  Vitamins — 122
  Antioxidants — 123
24-Hour Liver Flush — 124
  Ingredients — 126
  Directions — 127
  How Well Did You Do? — 131
  Congratulations — 132
  Take Action! — 132
Permanent and Fast Allergy Elimination — 132
Cleansing the Lymph — 134
Rebuilding the Adrenal Glands — 135
Cleansing the Fat — 135
Hubbard Sauna Protocol — 136

Table of Contents   XI

Dental Clean-Up	137
Chelation	137
Feeling Clean on the Inside	138

Chapter 7
Pain Elimination 139

Biochemical Causes of Pain	140
My Sulfur Miracle (MSM)	142
Acute Pain? Traumeel to the Rescue!	143
Structural Pain: Feet	144
Alignment of the Feet	145
Flat Feet	146
Improving Our Feet	148
Structural Pain: Hips	152
Structural Pain: Structural Alignment	154
Kyphosis	154
Lordosis	154
Scoliosis	154
The Root Cause of Back Issues	155
NeuroCranial Restructuring	156
Posture Makes Perfect	160
Energetic Pain	161
Life Without Pain	162

Chapter 8
Terminally Well 165

Immediate Life-Threatening Conditions	166
EBOO	167
Fasting and Juice Fasting	167
Master Cleanse	168
Gerson Protocol	170
Dr. Hulda Clark's 21-Day Cancer Elimination Program	171
Life-Long Conditions	172
My Dad's Story	173
Diabetes	174
Obesity	175
Are Any Diseases Truly Incurable?	175
Becoming Terminally Well	176

Chapter 9
Pay it Forward: Mastering the Art of Wellness — **177**
Epilogue — **181**
Conventional Wisdom? — 181
  The Truth — 182
  Positive Signs of Truth — 184
  Scientific Proof and Double-Blind Studies — 186
Take Control of Your Wealth — 187
Where Credit Is Due... — 188
Freedom of Choice — 189
Further Resources — **191**

Foreword

It is my pleasure and my privilege to be involved with this book, and I am delighted to have been asked by Craig to write this foreword.

As a naturopathic doctor, I am encouraged when I see any work that introduces naturopathic treatments to a wider audience and I am particularly pleased to see a book which looks at such a comprehensive range of treatments while putting the information into a context that makes it helpful for the reader.

This is a bold book which seeks to address illness without preconception. It looks from the patient's perspective and asks the simple question: what works? It doesn't ask what works within one particular field or what works according to one practitioner, but what works and what will improve the health of the patient. Craig has tried nearly all of the therapies in the book and with this experience he identifies solutions with proven clinical results and offers them to you.

Despite his experience in these matters, Craig understands the limitations of all of our knowledge, and like the best of us, remains a student. His web forum to share ideas and his advice to work with trained naturopathic physicians and other registered health practitioners both demonstrate his desire to keep learning and not to rely solely on self-diagnosis.

This book is an excellent resource and I recommend it to everyone.

Dr. Lorne Swetlikoff, ND

Lorne Swetlikoff, ND is a licensed naturopathic physician and current president of the College of Naturopathic Physicians of British Columbia.

Introduction

When it comes to healthcare, the US leads the developed world.

It has the highest incidence of heart disease, prostate cancer, breast cancer, colorectal cancer, and diabetes. According to US census statistics, there are over 700,000 doctors in the US, spending over one-trillion dollars (that's US $1,000,000,000,000). Sometimes it seems that the more money that is spent on healthcare, the less healthy we become.

How Do You Feel About Your Health?

So how do you feel about your health? Do you often feel stressed out or run down? When you look in the mirror do you feel unhappy with aspects of your appearance? Do you suffer from chronic pain or a more serious condition? What nagging health concerns are bothering you right now?

If there were affordable and reliable ways to quickly break free from these difficulties, would you keep an open mind and listen? If so, then you're ready to take control of your health and you can look forward to rewarding benefits, such as:

- freedom from pain and symptoms of disease
- waking up full of energy and optimism
- breaking free from feelings of depression and anxiety
- receiving compliments on your appearance, and
- not only losing weight, but also looking younger as the toxins clear from your body and your skin regains its elasticity.

You can soon stand out as a living example of how healthy a person can be, in stark contrast to those who eat a standard American diet or habitually smoke cigarettes and/or drink alcohol. But people in these latter two groups are not beyond repair by any stretch of the imagination—indeed, they actually have the most to gain!

My Story: Why Did I Get Interested In My Health?

Now that I have taken control of my health, I enjoy life so much more. However, my health was not always good.

I lived a happy, healthy childhood and spent a lot of time playing outdoors with friends. In high school, I played a lot of sports and wanted to be "cool" so when I started to get acne, I took tetracycline for several months to clear my skin. I then went on to university, where I had lots of fun, partying often and paying little attention to my health.

Then, at the age of twenty-one, my health fell apart. I experienced a couple of accidents that left me with chronic neck and back pain. I lived with chronic anxiety and even my libido began to deteriorate. In my despair, I wondered if I had AIDS because I was always getting sick, my skin was plagued with acne and frequent cold sores, and it would take weeks for even minor cuts and scratches to heal.

To deal with my health issues I visited numerous doctors, specialists, chiropractors, physiotherapists, and psychologists. At one point, I remember feeling overwhelmed with depression and I thought I'd never be healthy again. Maybe you can relate to this. Then after exhausting what conventional medicine had to offer, I began looking for alternatives. Soon after, I met an exceptional health practitioner named Nigel Jeffers, who became my Obi-Wan Kenobi, getting me started on the right path. As he explained to me, his role represented 10% of my healing process and the other 90% was up to me.

Nigel introduced me to naturopathic medicine, and not long after I visited the clinic of the exceptional Dr. Lorne Swetlikoff, ND, where I underwent a series of tests which uncovered that I had severe acidosis as well as candidiasis and leaky gut syndrome. All of these conditions are bad, but leaky gut was the worst. My digestive tract was leaking, and everything I consumed effectively became toxic to my system because of these leaks. When undigested food leaks into the blood stream, the liver quickly becomes overloaded and the immune system is forced to work at full capacity, 24/7, leaving no resources available to fight any cold or other illness that is going around. This leaky gut diagnosis helped explain my challenged immune system and with this understanding, I was able to take some positive action to change my situation.

Over the next 10 years I invested over a million dollars traveling the world and researching advanced health and performance enhancing technologies. I've tried dozens of therapies, including:

- several different nutrition protocols
- massage therapies
- podiatry
- personal training
- Rolfing

- the Alexander Technique
- naturopathic medicine
- homeopathic medicine
- osteopathic medicine
- visceral manipulation
- applied kinesiology
- colon hydrotherapy
- hydrogen peroxide therapy
- ozone therapy
- hyperbaric oxygen therapy
- acupuncture
- biofeedback
- aromatherapy
- reflexology
- crainosacral therapy
- NeuroCranial Restructuring®
- stretching
- yoga
- qigong
- meditation

- reiki
- BodyTalk
- ThetaHealing™
- flower essences and other vibrational remedies
- Emotional Freedom Techniques® (EFT)
- Tapas Acupressure Technique
- Resonance Repatterning®
- timeline therapy
- hypnotism
- Atlas Profilax®
- The Hubbard Sauna Protocol
- ayahuasca

...and more. Every therapist I visited and every book I read taught me something new about getting healthy. Progressively, my health has improved, and today I am happier and healthier than I've ever been.

My chronic pain has disappeared, my immune system is strong, and my chronic symptoms have vanished. Today, I'm more energetic, and best of all, my mental and emotional states have improved. I now have far greater mental clarity, and chronic anxiety and depression are things of the past. My self-confidence has returned and I truly feel like I've got a new lease on life.

Although it took me a few years to recover fully, an easier and faster path is now clear to me. By compiling the most fundamental concepts from each conventional and alternative therapy, I'm offering you the shortcuts to super-charge your health. Years of clinical research have proven each one of these shortcuts to be easy and effective.

You're unlikely to find these solutions brought together for you in any other single book. Most authors are experts in a single field and are not only biased to their field but also inexperienced with most other treatments. For instance, a massage therapist may be brilliant at releasing your painful muscles but is likely unable to explain why your muscles feel painful in the first place or how to correct the true cause. As I've been through most treatments, I can bring a broader perspective through this book.

Pointing Fingers

Let me make it clear that it is not my intent to point fingers at either side of the healthcare debate—my concern is to ensure that you find the right option to achieve the level of well-being you desire.

Today's conventional doctors practicing medicine are, in my experience, very bright and well-intentioned. Unfortunately, it has become clear that, as in most industries, corporate interests have hijacked the medical industry and put profits before people. As a result, medical doctors are educated and employed by a system that does not necessarily serve the best interests of the end consumer: the patient.

I think we're all aware of some of the limitations of conventional medicine. For instance:

- It is well-known how much damage conventional cancer cures can inflict on the body. Both radiation and chemotherapy can have a devastating effect, leaving the immune system shot to pieces, hair falling out, and the patient feeling worse than before the treatment started.

- Side effects are common to virtually all pharmaceutical drugs. Most people are aware of the serious birth defects attributed to the drug Thalidomide, which was prescribed to many pregnant women during the 1950s and 1960s. More recently, drugs like Vioxx have captured a great deal of attention because of their harmful effects.

- Equally, looking at mental health-related medicine, there is the famous Rosenhan experiment where a group of sane patients faked auditory hallucinations in order to gain access to 12 different psychiatric hospitals. Once inside, these patients—who were sane—behaved normally. The fake patients were diagnosed with schizophrenia (and one with manic-depression). All of the fake patients were discharged with a diagnosis of schizophrenia "in remission" after a stay of between 7 and 52 days.

Now don't get me wrong—I'm not trying to suggest one approach is better than the other. On the other side of the picture, away from conventional medicine, there is alternative or complementary medicine, and simply jumping into that blindly, without any due diligence, is potentially hazardous. The reasons are the same: while most people are well-intentioned, they are also trying to earn a living. In other words, while they may be giving you the truth, they may not be giving you the whole truth. Examples of this include overstating the claims of a product or citing some exceptional case studies where the treatment was extremely effective.

On both sides, but particularly with alternative options, there is a tendency to self-diagnose and to self-medicate without taking appropriate advice. The following comment may seem strange in a book which offers so many solutions, but to be clear and state explicitly: whether you follow a conventional or alternative course of treatment, it is always important to seek out suitably qualified and experienced practitioners when you are looking for a diagnosis. If nothing else, a naturopathic physician can run a batch of laboratory tests which can speed a diagnosis, and for instance identify not simply that you are nutrient deficient, but identify which specific nutrients you lack. On the flip side, it is important to make sure you are as well-informed as possible before you see any practitioner. This way you can understand the advice and question the approach that is being recommended for your treatment.

While it's easy to be critical, I don't want to point fingers at the healthcare system as a whole because if you peek behind the veil of any established industry, you'll see that there's the same tendency to lose sight of the truth in an effort to maximize profits. In other words, after looking closely at any established system, you tend to find that it is not working towards its stated purpose.

Fortunately, thorough investigation has revealed that, given the right information and encouragement, everyone can be their own best healer. If you believe that you deserve better health—and you're given the information you need to make a change—healing is not a difficult process. In fact, it's easy and affordable to improve our health.

What Now?

If you are ready to Take Control of Your Health, let me be the first to welcome you to a level of wellness that you may not have experienced for years.

This book presents information for you to follow at your own pace and helps you assess your progress every step of the way. If, in the course of this book, you find anything that is a burden or doesn't resonate with you, take a break and re-evaluate. This is not a race, unless you are terminally ill, in which case I would jump right to chapter 8.

If you haven't done so already, I suggest you check out our forums at Forums.CraigBrockie.com where you can find help, support, and a lively discussion about the issues covered in this book and many other issues beyond.

I will introduce you to approaches that make it easy for you to make positive changes. For instance, I will introduce you to the Internal Body Wash and the 24-Hour Liver Flush. I will talk about some of the main bacteria, viruses, and parasites that we all carry in our bodies, but which ultimately harm our well-being. Of course, I will tell you how you can eliminate these bacteria, viruses, and parasites, and ensure they do not return. As far as possible, I will identify approaches that automate the process or which you can integrate into your everyday routine. By keeping you motivated and helping you eliminate possible self-sabotaging behaviors, I will make sure that you stop tripping yourself up, so you can progress without falling off the wagon.

As well as looking at how you can improve your health now, this book also introduces you to other approaches that you might consider in the future, in particular if you contract an acute or chronic disease such as HIV, Hepatitis C, or cancer.

To keep this book manageable and easy to read, I've purposely avoided going into excessive technical detail in order to give you a concise overview of as many helpful topics as possible. As a supplement to this book, you will see that I have included as many references as I can to books, websites, treatments, practitioners, and films. Rather than follow each of these links individually, you can go to CraigBrockie.com/TakeControl and find all the links there for you. Not only that, but if any of the links have changed since publication, or if I've found anything new that I think you would be interested to know about, it will all be there. I highly recommend you visit this web page as soon as possible.

Like most things, the more a person studies the subject of wellness, the more they realize there is always more to learn and I continue to study the subject and regularly consult with accredited health care practitioners. I highly recommend you adopt this behavior too.

Before we go any further, let's assess your health now. Refer to the next page for details.

Winners Keep Score: Assessment

Before we begin, let's take a quick inventory of your health. Please take 90 seconds right now to complete the following assessment so we know your starting point and can identify the areas where you can expect the most improvement.

Please indicate how strongly you agree with the statements below, 0 being complete disagreement and 10 being absolute agreement.

Disagree «—» Agree

Physical Health

I am free from pain/symptoms:	0 1 2 3 4 5 6 7 8 9 10
I am fit and enjoy high energy levels:	0 1 2 3 4 5 6 7 8 9 10
I look healthy (weight, skin, hair):	0 1 2 3 4 5 6 7 8 9 10

Mental Health

I am easily able to concentrate:	0 1 2 3 4 5 6 7 8 9 10
I learn new things easily:	0 1 2 3 4 5 6 7 8 9 10
I have a great memory:	0 1 2 3 4 5 6 7 8 9 10

Emotional Health

I have high self esteem:	0 1 2 3 4 5 6 7 8 9 10
I am free from anxiety/worry:	0 1 2 3 4 5 6 7 8 9 10
I am free from depression/sadness:	0 1 2 3 4 5 6 7 8 9 10

The most important specific health challenge I would like to overcome is: _____

_____

My status with overcoming this challenge: 0 1 2 3 4 5 6 7 8 9 10
What it would mean to me to overcome this challenge:

_____
_____

Thank you for completing this assessment. You are a winner! Now let's focus on how to quickly, safely, and affordably move you further towards 10 in all of the areas in this assessment.

14   **Take Control of Your Health**

Chapter 1
Rinse Yourself Out

If you are like most people, you probably shower every day or at least a few times per week. Cleaning the outside of the body is a relatively simple process that most of us have mastered by an early age and do without thinking.

Cleaning the inside of our bodies, however, is a process that most of us don't often consider. Perhaps we assume that our body's built-in systems take care of that for us. Well, our bodies do have fantastic detoxification systems built-in, and if we were living a hundred years ago, internal cleaning may not have been such an important consideration.

However, in the 21st century, we live in a high-paced, high-stress world that's loaded with chemicals and toxins, harmful electromagnetic fields, and persuasive suggestions to consume oh-so-tasty but not-so-healthy foods and drinks. Although this book goes far beyond internal cleaning, the removal of some of the most toxic substances from our bodies is a great place to start.

Human Toxicity

Leading experts acknowledge that human toxicity has become the norm rather than the exception. While it is common for toxic overload to undermine one's health as a whole, many toxins have their own signature or effect on the body. For instance:

- Formaldehyde—which we're exposed to from indoor carpeting—competes with normal liver function.

- Xenoestrogens—which we are exposed to from plastics—are known to disrupt a person's natural hormone balance.

- Heavy metals are another huge contributor to ill health. To give some examples, lead often contributes to depression, mercury from immunizations is commonly found in children with autism, and aluminum toxicity is found in many patients with Alzheimer's and dementia.

If you're feeling depressed or stressed out, I have good news for you. If you need coffee to get going in the morning or "energy drinks" to keep going throughout the day, I have good news for you, too. Even if chronic pain and symptoms of disease have been plaguing you for years, I also have good news for you.

The good news is that it's as simple and affordable to clean out the inside of your body as it is to clean the outside, and as soon as this process begins, you're going to start feeling a whole lot better.

And here's the best part—it doesn't even require self-discipline. How does that sound to you? Well, let's jump right in and get started!

Toxic Build-Up

If you own a car, you know that it's a bad idea to run the engine in any enclosed space as the build-up of toxic fumes coming out of the tailpipe can be fatal. Some of the most toxic substances in our bodies come out of our tail pipe and we want to make sure that these toxins make a regular exit rather than accumulate in our system. According to naturopathic medicine, optimal health requires that a person eliminate at least twice, preferably three times daily.

How many times do you eliminate per day? Many people eliminate only once per day, and if that's the case, there's no cause for immediate concern. There are simple and affordable ways to correct this and you're going to feel great benefits from becoming more regular.

A person of optimal health eliminates three times

per day, usually after each meal. Picture the entire digestive system as a conveyor belt. Food goes in, moves the digestive tract along, and shortly afterwards, the person eliminates.

The colon has the capacity to hold several pounds of toxic waste. The body's waste not only contains the toxins we've consumed but often serves as a breeding ground for harmful bacteria, viruses, and parasites.

The colon is the body's primary channel of elimination, which is why we want to make sure our colon is functioning optimally before we begin any further detoxification processes. In other words, there's no sense loosening up the stored toxins in our organs and the other areas of our bodies if the toxins can't then make a quick exit.

As Jon Barron explains in his book *Lessons from the Miracle Doctors* (Basic Health Publications, 2008), the real cause behind sickness and disease is often the retention and re-absorption of built-up toxic waste as our largest internal organ—the liver—filters dangerous poisons from the body and passes them out through the colon. Plug the colon, and it's like flushing a toilet that's clogged: everything backs up.

So, as a result of a clogged colon, the liver becomes compromised, which compromises health systems further up the chain, manifesting in whichever parts of our bodies are our weakest links. It all starts in the colon though, and that's why this book starts by explaining how to effectively and affordably clean out the colon.

Let's Get Moving!

If you're currently eliminating fewer than three times daily, you will find benefits in increasing your water consumption. Next, visit your local health food store to pick up a bottle of vitamin C, a magnesium supplement, and a box of herbal laxative tea. Begin taking the vitamin C and magnesium daily as directed on the bottle. In addition to encouraging regularity, both products provide excellent systemic benefits that we will discuss later in this book

Start by making a cup of tea each night and drink half before bed and the other half when you wake up in the morning (one tea bag per day). If, after a couple of days, you're still not eliminating three times daily, increase to a full cup before bed and another full cup upon awakening (two tea bags per day). Continue until the box is finished. If two bags per day still doesn't achieve the results we're aiming for, try introducing more fiber into your diet. For this purpose, ground flax seeds or psyllium husks are good additions to breakfast cereal or smoothies.

Herbal laxative teas are formulated not only to stimulate the colon and increase the number of bowel movements you have each day, but also to begin to loosen the compacted waste along the walls of your colon that has built up over the years. If your budget allows, using an oxygenating colon cleansing product like OxyFlush instead of herbal laxative tea is an excellent option.

You will notice in the next few chapters that I am a big fan of magnesium (for many reasons, which I will explain). Magnesium has a loosening effect on the body—it helps muscles relax and also has a relaxing effect on the bowel, so you will find that if you take magnesium it will have the added benefit of keeping you moving. Vitamin C helps tissue rebuild, provides excellent antioxidant benefits, and also has a loosening effect on the bowels.

Now Rinse

How would you like to give your body a shower from the inside out?

There are a few ways to put your colon on the rinse cycle using water to flush it out. If you have the time, money, and desire to do a series of colonic irrigations to rinse out your colon, consider researching colon hydrotherapy and look for a service provider in your area. However, if you don't want to drive across town to colonic appointments that will end up costing you a few hundred dollars, or if the thought of having water forced into your colon doesn't appeal to you, I've got another solution which I personally prefer.

This solution not only rinses out your colon with

water but also cleans your entire digestive tract. I call it the Internal Body Wash and you'll want to do a series of about ten of these on days as close together as your schedule allows.

The Internal Body Wash involves drinking a cup of herbal laxative tea at bedtime and consuming an appetizing, but salty broth first thing in the morning. Why salty? Well, first we need to discuss the term specific gravity.

Perhaps you already know that you can't drink sea water to quench your thirst. This is mainly because salt water has a similar specific gravity to that of our blood. So instead of being absorbed into our bodies to hydrate us, salt water passes right on through. This is bad news if you're stranded at sea; however, it is good news if you want to rinse out your digestive system using the Internal Body Wash.

Internal Body Wash Step 1: Ingredients

The first step is to visit your local health food store to pick up a box of herbal laxative tea (if you haven't already got some) and some sea salt.

Internal Body Wash Step 2: Making the Broth

Start the day by boiling some water. In a large measuring cup, add two measured teaspoons of sea salt and one quart of hot water (one teaspoon is 5ml and one quart is equivalent to 0.95 liters). You can also add a few dashes of your favorite herbs for flavor. Try using flavorful but mild herbs instead of spicy ones to ensure your comfort. Let your salty broth sit for a few minutes until it is cool enough to consume or add a few ice cubes.

Internal Body Wash Step 3: Consuming the Broth

In one sitting, drink the salty broth you've just made. This should be the first thing you consume on this day, other than perhaps a small glass of water on awakening if you were feeling dehydrated. Whether you drink your broth from a mug or use a bowl and spoon, it doesn't matter—just finish it all in one sitting. If you like salt, you'll love the taste. If not, feel free to sip small amounts of water to clear your mouth.

Internal Body Wash Step 4: The Rinse Cycle

Now, wait as the (herbal) salt water works its way through your stomach and into your intestines. While most people experience no concerns, if you have a sensitive stomach or are prone to nausea, you may find comfort in enjoying a few deep and relaxed breaths while gently rubbing your stomach. A small piece of candied ginger may also be comforting.

If you've got something to do around the house, go to it. The entire rinse process takes a while, so you'll want to do this on a day when you will be awake for about two hours before leaving the house because it can take up to an hour for the salt water to begin exiting your body.

Internal Body Wash Step 5: Repeat

If you're short on time, drinking just the broth will flush out the majority of the contents of your colon and get you on with your day sooner. For a more thorough rinsing, you can start drinking large glasses of fresh water about 30 to 40 minutes after you finish the broth. Repeat the glasses of fresh water every 10 to 20 minutes thereafter. This will extend the rinse cycle, moving more water through you. You'll find that, within a few minutes of downing another big glass or two of water, more water will keep showering through. Use room temperature water (not too cold) to assure your comfort.

Internal Body Wash: Reactions and Results

The Internal Body Wash works best for those who have their bowels moving two or more times daily. Those who are chronically constipated (one or fewer bowel movements daily) will benefit from following the suggestions earlier in this chapter before attempting the Internal Body Wash.

In the unlikely event that you do not experience results from the Internal Body Wash, remember that no two people are exactly alike. If you did not get results on your first attempt, it is probably due to skipping the herbal laxative tea the night before, not starting the morning with an absolutely empty stomach, or drinking fresh water too soon after finishing the broth. You might also try adjusting the amount of sea salt you use, trying slightly more or slightly less. Take these things into consideration and try again.

I've also had success inducing an Internal Body Wash by beginning the day with 2 to 3 teaspoons of vitamin C powder followed by several glasses of fresh water. Taking enough magnesium at one time can also induce loose enough bowels to initiate an Internal Body Wash.

The Internal Body Wash was inspired by the "Salt Water Flush" found in *The Master Cleanser* by Stanley Burroughs (Burroughs Books, 1976). If you're a purist, The Master Cleanser calls for using lukewarm water instead of hot water and sea salt without your favorite herbs for flavor. I think you'll find The Internal Body Wash recipe equally effective and far more palatable.

Internal Body Wash: Cycle Finished

Congratulations!

You've just rinsed out your colon and entire digestive tract! You'll likely feel a lot more energetic for the rest of the day, especially if you avoid eating heavy meals. Try easing your digestive system back into action with a glass of freshly squeezed juice. Eating raw fruit, seeds, nuts, and vegetables for the remainder of the day will keep your energy levels high.

While juicing and eating raw produce might not sound appealing to you now, I assure you that the more you clean out your body, the more your body will crave foods that are good for you and the less you will crave "junk" food.

Chlorinated Water

On the topic of water, although the bottled water industry has convinced us that it's unsafe to drink chlorinated tap water, most people have no idea that we absorb more chlorine through our skin and lungs in a ten-minute shower than if we were to drink unfiltered tap water all day.

I highly recommend investing an hour of your time to install a whole-house charcoal water filter. For under $50, most major hardware stores sell kits (these include friction fittings, so you can easily install the filter yourself without needing a plumber).

The good part about these systems is that replacement filters are less than $10 and last about three months. In chapter 2, I'll share another affordable secret to improve your water, but the simple installation of a charcoal filter will make a big difference in many aspects of your health and life. Not only will your water be safer to drink and better tasting, but by showering in non-chlorinated water your hair will be softer, your skin less dry, and your immune system and detoxification organs will appreciate you taking the load off.

If you don't own your own property, or are unable to install a whole-house filter, a shower head filter is another option.

Integrating the Internal Body Wash into Your Daily Routine

It is ideal to complete ten colonic irrigations or Internal Body Washes as quickly as your schedule allows.

As you use the Internal Body Wash more, you'll find it's a great way to counter the effects of a night of over-indulgence. Not only is it a great hangover cure, but it also feels fantastic the morning after a holiday feast.

Now Your Colon's Clean...

Cleaning your colon is the first step on the road to better health. In later chapters, you'll learn how easy and affordable it is to:

- kill the viruses that antibiotics can't touch
- rid yourself of parasites
- bolster your immune system, and
- flush out your liver—both your digestion and

ability to process alcohol will be renewed, thus helping you further avoid the suffering associated with being human.

We'll also look at:

- How to quickly overcome chronic pain and correct the actual causes of your pain, rather than simply hiding it with medication.

- How easy it is to overcome depression and anxiety, and learn ways to stop cravings in their tracks so that even when you get the urge to eat something you consider "bad," you can easily avoid doing so... if that's what you want.

Remember, this book isn't about being hard on yourself. Quite the opposite: you're being given all the shortcuts and secrets to affordably optimize your health and you are encouraged to follow the path at your own pace. There's no need to beat yourself up or stress out about disciplining yourself. Learn to love yourself and accept that you're human.

So are you ready to take the next step toward taking control of your health?

Chapter 2
How Are You Feeling?

It is widely understood that stress and our emotional state both have a major impact on our physical health and well-being. The reality of dealing with the problems we all face in our everyday lives—such as a mountain of debt, ill health, challenging relationships, too much to do in too little time, past traumas, anxiety, or all of the above—can make inner peace and happiness seem unattainable. I know I felt this way at one time.

Many people tend to see their feelings as stemming from their physical health—if their health is "bad" then they have an expectation that they will feel "bad". Equally, many people see their emotional condition as being determined by outside events. However, the reverse is also true—we can take control of our health and take control of the outside events we experience by taking control of our emotional state.

The Effect of the Mind on Health

Before we look at the actions we can take to improve how we feel, let's look at some of the effects that our mind can exert on our physical health.

The Placebo Phenomenon

You're probably familiar with the placebo effect, right? It's widely accepted that patients unknowingly prescribed a placebo commonly experience an improvement in their health based on their positive expectations alone. What most people don't realize is the placebo effect was found to be equally prevalent in patients who received "mock" surgeries. The placebo effect is so powerful that double-blind studies are considered necessary to provide scientific validation for any treatment protocol.

Personality Disorders

Another excellent example of the power of the mind can be seen in patients suffering from dissociative identity disorder (which used to be called multiple personality disorder). In Michael Talbot's book *The Holographic Universe* (Harper Perennial, 1992) he gives a fascinating example of a clinical study where a man with dissociative identity disorder had the "incurable" disease we call diabetes in only one of his identities. That's right, medical doctors confirmed the same man had diabetes at one moment but didn't the next (after he had undergone a change in identity).

Think about that for a moment. How many of us emotionally "own" the disease we've been diagnosed with as incurable and something we just have to live with for the rest of our lives?

Stress

There are many safe, affordable, and effective shortcuts to reducing stress and increasing happiness in our lives. Before we look at these, let's first look at some of the things that happen in our bodies when we're experiencing stress.

Among other detrimental effects, when we experience stress it is common for:

- our breathing to become shallow
- our blood pressure to increase
- our heart rate to become erratic, and
- our hormones to get out of balance.

Shallow Breathing

Shallow breathing reduces the amount of oxygen we absorb. Oxygen is arguably the most important requirement for our bodies. If you don't believe me, just hold your breath and see how long you make it.

Not only can we not survive without oxygen, but

cells deficient in oxygen become acidic and weak, creating an ideal environment for disease. Cancer, pain, viruses, parasites, harmful bacteria, and all other anaerobic microbes flourish in the absence of oxygen. As we'll discuss in the next chapter, we want to flood our bodies with oxygen, not deprive them.

Increased Blood Pressure and Erratic Heart Rate

Emotional stress also puts undue strain on the heart. Not only does our blood pressure increase when we are experiencing stress, but our heart rate variability becomes erratic, adding additional strain. With heart disease being such a common killer, reducing stress is more important than ever.

Raging Hormones

Hormones are a popular health topic these days. When it comes to wellness and stress, two hormones take center stage:

- dehydroepiandrosterone (DHEA), and
- cortisol.

DHEA is a healing hormone and of the two, it is the one we want to be dominant in our bodies. Cortisol increases blood pressure and blood sugar and suppresses immune response. When we are experiencing stress, cortisol overwhelms the body and suppresses DHEA levels, leaving us more susceptible to disease and reducing our ability to heal.

Results of a Stressful Lifestyle

When thinking about a stressful lifestyle and the implications that this may have for us, it is important to consider how excessive stress contributes to poor eating habits and poor life decisions. Even if we don't notice it in ourselves, we probably notice when other people make questionable life decisions when under stress. For instance, do you recognize any of these behaviors in the people you deal with in your everyday life?

- Taking out anger on a spouse, children, employees/co-workers, the dog, or getting angry at people in traffic.

- Smoking, drinking, taking drugs, overeating, gambling and other outlets to channel stress. Ironically, these "releases" end up creating more stress.

- Racking up credit card debt to buy something just to feel better.

Whether these examples apply to you or not, I'm sure you recognize the behavior. And I'm sure we all recognize how we can crave a bag of chips or container of ice cream when we're feeling stressed out. I found it interesting when it was pointed out that the word stressed spelled backward is desserts—of course it's got to be plural. And one of my favorite

Homer Simpson quotes is, "Ah beer. The cause of and solution to all of life's problems."

The Interrelation between Health and Stress

Now that we understand some of the physical effects of stress, let's briefly discuss the relationship between our emotions and specific conditions.

A good place to start is by considering the work of best-selling author and one of the founders of the self-help movement, Louise Hay. Hay has identified the specific emotions that relate to each disease. For instance:

- Pain usually relates to the feelings of guilt and a belief that one deserves to suffer.

- AIDS relates to feeling defenseless and hopelessness, and a feeling that nobody cares. Coupled with this is a strong belief in not being good enough, and denial of the self and sexual guilt.

- Cancer is usually found to correlate with a deep hurt, long-standing resentment, and a deep secret or grief that is eating away at the self.

Hay's book *You Can Heal Your Life* (Hay House, 2004) includes the related emotional patterns for all common diseases.

Since cancer is so common and deadly, let's dive

deeper into the big C and look at its relationship with our emotions. After twenty years of research and therapy with over 31,000 patients, Dr. Ryke Geerd Hamer from Germany has established firmly, logically, and empirically how cancer can be reversed and a patient returned to health, simply by assisting the patient in resolving deep rooted inner conflicts.

If you remain doubtful that thoughts, feelings, and beliefs can have such a predictable effect on the body, consider the work of cellular biologist, Bruce Lipton, PhD. In his book *The Biology of Belief* (Hay House, 2008), Lipton lays out exactly how the mind/body connection operates at the cellular level and how the environment we create for ourselves has far more influence on our health than the genetics we are born with.

Addressing Emotion-Related Illness

In the West, treatment of emotion-related illness is widely practiced and mainly consists of drug use and psychotherapy. There's little debating that drugs can be effective in reducing the symptoms of stress, at least while one is under their influence. Alcohol has been used for hundreds of years to help people relax and forget about their troubles. Many recreational drugs are also used to escape life for a while. While some are quick to judge alcoholics and narcotics abusers for self-medicating, it has become socially accepted for people to take prescription sleeping pills, anti-anxiety medications, and antidepressant drugs to cope with life. This approach to medication doesn't seem to be very different.

If you're feeling hopeless with depression or on the brink of a nervous breakdown, I'd like to congratulate you. You're experiencing a very strong signal that something is out of alignment in your life and you now have the motivation to change. You deserve to be happy, and I hope some of the suggestions in this chapter will help you as they have helped me and many others.

If you still feel overwhelmed after trying some of the non-drug solutions that follow, there are many competent professionals that can prescribe you a drug to give you relief. If you do choose to use prescription drugs, please consider approaching them as a stepping stone rather than looking to them as a permanent solution. Most people on antidepressant and anti-anxiety drugs continue to struggle with feelings of sadness and worry, which indicates these drugs are far from an ideal solution.

Personal Counseling Therapy

Psychotherapy is excellent if you can afford it, but at $150 or more per hour, many cannot. Fortunately, many tools such as self-hypnosis and cognitive therapies (as simple as keeping a journal or heart-to-heart conversations with a good friend or family member) can also be effective in dealing with stress.

One of my favorite mental health practices is keeping a journal. I learned of this technique from the excellent book, *The Feeling Good Handbook* by David D Burns (Plume, 1999) which teaches cognitive therapy. Cognitive therapy is all about becoming more objective about our emotions. I have voice recording software on my iPhone which I use for keeping a journal and I also keep a pad of paper for collecting my thoughts. The reason I find keeping a journal so effective is that I often find that I can be plagued with the same thoughts running through my head relentlessly until I capture them on paper. I find that by simply recording my thoughts, not only does the "hamster" constantly spinning on its wheel in my brain slow down, but the answers I've been looking for immediately become obvious.

Having a heart-to-heart talk with a close friend or family member is another excellent outlet. Just be careful and approach the conversation in a supportive and solution-oriented manner rather than a bitch-and-complain session. If you can afford a therapist, you might find the objectivity and privacy even better. I believe your results will be much faster, effortless and longer-lasting working with a skilled EFT, BodyTalk, or ThetaHealing practitioner, however conventional therapists are good too.

Energetic Medicine

I believe the field of energetic medicine shows the most promise for allowing us to take control of our mental and emotional health affordably and effectively. While less understood in the West, the body's energetic systems have been widely recognized for thousands of years in Eastern medicine.

The concept of energy is certainly not absent from Western medicine. For example, it is common for dieters and athletes to be obsessed with calories, which are a measurement of energy. Western medicine also makes use of energetic diagnostic equipment like EEG, ECG, and CT scans. There are also energetic treatments in Western medicine. For instance, lasers are commonly used in surgery and we can even kick start your heart with a defibrillator.

The Eastern Influence in Energetic Medicine

The Chinese mapped out the body's energy meridians over five thousand years ago. Gamma ray technology has recently proven these meridians actually do exist. Ancient Indian knowledge of the body's energy vortexes or chakras have also now been verified with modern biofeedback devices.

It has been said that emotion is simply energy-in-motion. I would agree with this statement and also add that negative emotions usually relate to stuck energy. Using a simple-to-learn acupressure

How Are You Feeling?   39

A computer-enhanced image of the meridian system picked out by a gamma camera after radioactive tracers had been injected into acupuncture points. This is the body's circuit board or meridian system. Energy is intended to flow freely through the entire system. When the system is short-circuited, it can manifest as illness. Source: *Infinite Love is the Only Truth— Everything Else is Illusion* (David Icke Books, 2005).

technique, we can quickly eliminate our negative emotions by removing our related energetic blockages. Once the energetic blockages are removed, the negative emotions usually subside, in many cases permanently. The best part is that the process often takes less than ten minutes to complete and is free.

Emotional Freedom Techniques

Emotional Freedom Techniques, or EFT for short, take less than 10 minutes to remove energetic blockages.

EFT has been clinically proven to be effective in quickly overcoming many symptoms of physical, mental, and emotional disease. I've witnessed demonstrations where veteran soldiers plagued with extreme symptoms of post-traumatic stress disorder have rapidly regained their emotional freedom in just one session. Rather than medicating or visiting a psychotherapist again and again to rehash the same trauma, EFT provides immediate and lasting results.

EFT is a great tool you can use at any time and for any reason to improve your emotional state. Whether you are trying to overcome an addiction, deal with a sudden craving, let go of a past trauma, overcome feelings of guilt and shame, or trying to stop worrying and start living, EFT is for you.

EFT was developed by Gary Craig, who simplified

the protocol of an earlier acupressure technique developed by Roger Callahan called TFT. By the way, I'm far from the only guy advocating the use of EFT—best-selling authors Jack Canfield, Bob Proctor, Kevin Trudeau, Joseph Mercola, and many others highly recommend the use of this wonderful free healing technique.

You can learn the basics of EFT by watching my free five-minute demonstration. Go to CraigBrockie.com/TakeControl to find the video and the other related resources mentioned in this chapter.

For more thorough study, go to emofree.com where you can download a free EFT manual. EFT really is simple to learn and remember and you'll be doing yourself a huge favor by adding EFT to your toolkit. Of course, EFT is just one of many energetic medicine techniques you can explore to improve your mental and emotional health. I will share other safe, affordable, and effective tools later in this chapter.

Magnesium

Magnesium has many applications. When addressing emotional health issues, magnesium has a relaxing effect on the body and emotions, which is especially beneficial for those who suffer anxiety.

Aromatherapy

You know how you might hear a song on the radio

that you haven't heard since you were in high school, and how hearing the song takes you back to a certain place in time? So can smells.

Maybe you had a friend in college who wore a certain perfume or cologne. You could be walking down the street and smell something that triggers the memory and boom!! You will be taken back to a place and a time, and a whole group of memories and feelings. You might remember everything about that friend and you might remember many other feelings and emotions associated with that time.

Aromatherapy as a concept always sounded very hippy-dippy, wishy-washy to me. But I have found, for emotion-related issues, it can be very effective.

Our sense of smell is far more sensitive than other senses and recognition of smell is immediate. Other senses like touch and taste must travel through the body via neurons and the spinal cord before reaching the brain, whereas the olfactory response passes directly to the brain.

Our sense of smell directly exposes our central nervous system to our environment. That is why inhalation directly affects the central nervous system. The olfaction response bypasses the neocortex, or conscious brain, and goes directly to the limbic system.

Smell is one of the strongest links to the subconscious and we retain memories associated with smells for very long periods of time.

There is a line of essential oils by a company called Young Living, and they have done the best job that I have found of coming up with different blends for improving emotional state. For instance, they have blends including:

- forgiveness
- joy
- present time

and many others. In other words, there is a range of blends to help with different aspects of our lives and different situations. Check out CraigBrockie.com/Feeling for a link to their product range.

The Raindrop Technique

The Raindrop Technique is an aromatherapy protocol that goes way beyond emotion-related illness, but I want to introduce it here because it is so powerful.

This is a massage therapy where lots of pungent oils such as oregano, thyme, and basil are spread down the spine so that the body picks them up through the massage. This balances the energy field, making us feel happier and more at ease, and reduces stress.

The Raindrop Technique also offers a huge benefit by boosting the immune system.

Tantra

People have hang-ups about a lot of things in their lives. For many people, sexual hang-ups are near the top of the list. Whether they've been abused, had sexual health problems, or simply feel uncertain about themselves, people do not talk openly about the issue. Our society talks a lot about sex when it wants to sell products, but we don't talk about sex in terms of relationships and intimacy. In many ways, talking about intimacy is a taboo topic—it's certainly not the kind of subject you would discuss at a dinner party.

Tantra helps to heal a person's feelings about their own sexuality and to feel more at ease with intimacy. Often this increased confidence can speed healing in other areas, too. Additionally, if practised the way it is intended, tantra boosts one's energy levels like few things can.

What Are You Believing?

Let's get back to the primary question of this chapter: how are you feeling? Or perhaps, more importantly, what are you believing?

Are we healthy or are we a victim of disease? Do we live in a friendly, abundant world or a hostile world of scarcity? Will we be able to handle what the future has in store for us or are we justified in living each day in fear? Do we truly love ourselves and enjoy a high self-esteem or are we somehow not deserving?

Are We Healthy or Are We a Victim of Disease?

Let's begin with whether we believe we are healthy or a victim of disease.

If you believe you are a victim of disease, I'm afraid there's no hope for you to take control of your health. So many people get caught in the trap of disease. The Western (allopathic) medical model is based on the treatment of symptoms. Every symptom is given a name to categorize it as a disease:

- Inflammation of the joints is labeled arthritis.
- Inflammation of the colon is labeled colitis.
- The body's inability to continue to deal with poor nutrition is labeled diabetes.

You get the idea.

Allopathic medicine specializes in providing drugs and surgery to suppress symptoms, in most cases without thoroughly addressing the underlying cause. As a result, Western medicine labels many diseases as incurable because the diseases *are* incurable under that model of treatment. Therefore, when people are diagnosed with diseases—which can be as absurd as restless leg syndrome—they have a tendency to accept the disease as a life sentence and their mentality becomes that of a victim. In reality, most diseases that allopathic medicine labels as incurable are anything but.

Do We Live in a Friendly, Abundant World or a Hostile World of Scarcity?

Albert Einstein has been credited with many profound statements. My personal favorite is: "The most important decision we make is whether we believe we live in a friendly or hostile universe."

What do you believe?

If we buy into the fear-based negativity propagated in the news each day, it's easy to assume we live in a cruel, hostile world. But again, what is truth and what is fiction? Aren't most people rather friendly and helpful when called upon? Cruel, hostile people seem to be more of the exception than the rule, don't they?

Let's talk about abundance for a moment. Scarcity has been falsely propagated upon humanity for millennia. Entire nations were once duped into believing that sodium chloride was scarce enough to justify accepting salt in exchange for one's labor. This is the origin for the word salary. Today we would consider it ridiculous to work for salt since we realize how abundant it is, with two thirds of our planet covered in salt water.

At the same time, many of us are convinced there is a scarcity of time, money, fresh water, energy, and many other commodities. What is truth and what is fiction? Do we really live in a world of scarcity or do we just have resource mismanagement issues we need to address?

Are We Justified in Living Each Day In Fear?

Now let's talk about fear. I am something of an expert on this one as I come from a long line of worriers and have lived with chronic anxiety for a great deal of my life.

One thing that is important to realize is that fear is always about the future. If you keep a journal—which is something I highly recommend—then it's easy to look back at previous entries about worrisome events that never manifested. In fact, most of what we worry about never happens. Now open a fresh page in your journal and write down what you're worried about right now. I bet that within minutes you'll feel much calmer as the upsetting thoughts that have been running non-stop in your mind are replaced with more positive thoughts, and solutions magically come to you. Understanding and putting into action the wisdom found in the book *Feel the Fear and Do It Anyway* by Susan Powers (Ballantine Books, 2006) is also a good plan if you're prone to worry.

Do We Truly Love Ourselves?

The feelings of guilt, shame, and low self-esteem are other silent killers, sapping us not only of our health, but our happiness. It seems like the best way to overcome issues with our past is to accept, forgive and forget. But why is it that it seems so much easier to accept and forgive others than it is ourselves? How do we go from being our own worst enemy to becoming our own best friend?

What makes things even more challenging is that it is very common to think one thing consciously but subconsciously believe the opposite. For instance, while we may think that we deserve to be healthy, we may subconsciously believe we deserve to suffer. These beliefs may stem from a past experience we still feel guilty about. Until our inner conflict is resolved and we get our conscious and subconscious in alignment, the body will have difficultly healing.

Applied Kinesiology

Using a simple biofeedback technique called Applied Kinesiology, or muscle testing, it is easy to determine if our subconscious mind would benefit from reprogramming.

Those familiar with muscle testing know that muscle strength is affected by what we think and say. If we focus on or say a truthful statement, our muscles remain strong. If we think or say a statement that we believe to be false on any level of consciousness, our muscles become measurably weaker. Test yourself on statements such as:

- I deserve to be healthy.
- I deserve to be happy.
- I deserve to suffer.

The results may shock you. Fortunately, it is easy to reprogram the subconscious mind. For those unfamiliar with Applied Kinesiology, check out CraigBrockie.com/Feeling where you can find several short videos demonstrating this effective, free technique.

EFT, BodyTalk, and ThetaHealing

If you're not the do-it-yourself type and are blessed with sufficient abundance to invest a few hundred dollars in your health, you'll be happy to know that a skilled EFT, BodyTalk, or ThetaHealing practitioner can quickly help you uncover and release sources of inner conflict which arise from the conscious and subconscious minds being out of alignment. When these conflicts are gone, you will not only feel greater emotional freedom, but often physical symptoms improve. Go to CraigBrockie.com/Practitioners where you can find links to qualified energetic healing practitioners.

Fasting... from the News and External Distractions

On the topic of the subconscious mind, one of the best pieces of advice I have ever implemented came from Dr. Andrew Weil. He suggested taking what he called a "news fast." It is my opinion that the news has one main purpose and that is to keep our attention by telling us what to be afraid of day after day. What other reason is there for propagating the worst of the worst of what's going on in the world on a given day?

I'm of the no-news-is-good-news camp and since I began tuning out the news, my life has been much happier. In fact, I've taken this concept much further and do my best to tune out as much television as possible. The reason for this is simple: while not all television programs are bad, almost all commercials are of very low integrity. Most advertisements are not only extremely misleading, but they communicate the message that we are somehow incomplete or not good enough, which is very detrimental to our self-image and self-esteem. If that's not bad enough, these sophisticated commercials are designed primarily to communicate to our subconscious mind while we are "zoned out" and relaxing in a very susceptible, almost hypnotic state as we wait for our program to return.

I even take "computer fasts" each weekend to allow me to focus on enjoying time with my family. I also suggest becoming more aware of cell phone texting and mobile email addictions as other distractions from being present and enjoying life. If your BlackBerry is better described as a Crackberry, or you find yourself interrupted by text messages regularly throughout your day, consider turning your mobile device off—or at least putting it on mute—now and then.

Voltage

Getting back to energy, let's talk about our voltage for a moment.

I think the movie *Monsters Inc.* offers an interesting portrayal of how our collective energy is managed by fear. That said, the movie *The Matrix* probably offers the best image of human bodies serving as an energy source. The truth is that whether we feel energetic or not, our bodies are teeming with energy. To illustrate this point, we all know we consume food, which is measured in calories, and if we happened to find ourselves trapped in a cage with a hungry lion, we'd prove to be a rich caloric (energy) source.

Nobel Prize winner Otto Warburg found that healthy cells in the body have a voltage of 70mV or higher. He also identified that aged cells have a voltage of about 50mV and that cancer cells have a voltage of 15mV or lower. Keeping our bodies in a high energy state and keeping the energy balanced and flowing throughout the entire body is therefore important.

Supercharge Your Life with Sacred G

I've invested well over $100,000 into various energy medicine technologies. My absolute favorite of all for boosting and balancing one's energy is called Sacred G and it's a unique system that works while you sleep.

You simply put Sacred G under your bed and the technology does the rest. Immediately you begin experiencing far more vivid dreams and your dream recall upon waking is greatly enhanced. This is the first indication that the Sacred G is working as you process more emotions than you normally would in your sleep. Soon after, users begin to experience a noticeable boost in energy, reduced stress levels, and more happiness.

I started out with two cases of Sacred G and my life has never been the same since. I gradually built myself up to 72 cases and it's difficult to imagine life without them. Sacred G not only helps balance and charge users, but it also automates the self-development process and even helps eliminate self-sabotaging behaviors. For instance, I've been working on this book for several years now and Sacred G has helped give me the boost and focus I needed to finally get it done.

Enhancing Your Household Water Supply

Sacred G can also be used to charge up your drinking water.

In the last chapter I suggested installing a whole-house charcoal filtration system and mentioned I'd be sharing another secret to enhance your drinking water in this chapter, and this is it. All you do is apply Sacred G to your hot water tank and near each faucet in your home. The technology energetically restructures the water with results that are obvious to everyone. In fact, after just 30 minutes of exposure to Sacred G, the taste and texture of water is noticeably improved when compared with water from the same source that has not been exposed to the technology. Not only is the water smoother, and with a better taste, but it is more bioavailable to the body.

I love this technology so much that I felt compelled to develop a humanitarian campaign to introduce a free sample of Sacred G to be used to help neutralize the harmful effects of the electromagnetic field (EMF) pollution that cell phones emit. This is not the primary application for Sacred G, but independent scientific trials, including double-blind studies, have proven the technology to be effective.

Visit FreeShield.com to get the free sample of Sacred G for your cell phone. At that site you'll also learn how the technology works and find links to free samples you can try under your pillow to begin charging yourself up while you sleep.

Those who are sensitive to subtle energy, such as advanced yoga students, Reiki masters, and Traditional Chinese Doctors will notice the effects from just one sample of Sacred G. Others may require several copies of the free sample to notice the effects. Absolutely everyone I've tested Sacred G with notices the positive effects when several cases are used.

Electromagnetic Field Pollution

The topic of EMF pollution is also very important to understand. Another reason I developed the FreeShield.com campaign is to promote awareness and educate people about the detrimental effects of EMF pollution.

Nowadays we are bombarded by unnatural frequencies and fields that didn't exist just twenty years ago. Most people now carry a cell phone, use a cordless phone and wireless internet at home, and have a digital alarm clock sitting next to their bed. Add to this the radio waves, microwaves, satellite signals, and who knows what else is hitting us 24/7. It all makes for a very disruptive energetic environment, which contributes to our stress levels. The good news is that there are many products available to remedy the situation, including of course, Sacred G, which I mentioned above.

Other Ways to Reduce Stress and Maximize Happiness

Now that we've talked about all that "woo woo" energetic stuff, let's talk about other methods to reduce our stress levels and maximize our happiness.

Naturopathic Medicine

Naturopathic medicine offers some of the best sources for fast relief of stress. For instance, the herb Kava Kava was instrumental in helping me get the upper hand on my anxiety. Those who suffer from anxiety or depression may want to research St. John's Wort, SAM-E, GABA and 5-HTP. Valerian is an excellent herb if you have difficulties falling asleep. Supplementing with high doses of B vitamins and magnesium, and completing a Candida reduction program are also helpful ideas to help reduce stress.

Vibrational Remedies

There are also many excellent homeopathic and vibrational remedies. For instance, a product I suggest for every glove box, first aid kit, and purse is called Rescue Remedy. Rescue Remedy offers immediate relief from most common upsets. I prefer the spray applicator over the dropper for ease of use.

Once Rescue Remedy has proven itself to you, you'll be excited to know that you can get customized vibrational remedies for your particular emotional needs. For instance, there are specific vibrational remedies for guilt, anxiety, phobias, and many other feelings. My friend Sasha Cuff has dedicated his life to developing vibrational remedies. You can contact this master practitioner directly through his NaturesSpirits.ca website. Sasha provides one-on-one telephone consultations and then prepares and mails your custom remedies to you.

Group Healing

Some of the most powerful and rapid emotional healing I've experienced has come through group healing sessions. There is something about working with a group with the common goal of emotional healing and self improvement. I think this is the main reason Alcoholics Anonymous has saved so many lives. The group experiences I've personally had the best results with are ayahuasca ceremonies and a seminar called *Challenge*.

Ayahuasca is a legal entheogen that has been used safely in Peru for centuries. Those who work with ayahuasca enter a lucid dream-like state, allowing them to vividly identify, come to terms with, and clear suppressed emotions and subconscious limitations. The experience is so profound and powerful that I equate a four-hour ceremony with several years of conventional therapy.

Challenge seminar is hosted by Carol Reynolds near Las Vegas. *Challenge* is an excellent seminar that goes far beyond textbook concepts. The focus of the seminar is moving participants beyond the emotional baggage that is preventing them from achieving what they are destined to achieve.

There are many excellent seminars focused on maximizing emotional health. Visit CraigBrockie.com/Feeling for information and recommendations.

Once you've started using one or more of the suggested therapies and remedies listed above, I expect you'll begin feeling calmer and happier soon after. Now let's take another step towards happiness and the Holy Grail, inner peace.

Headphone Sessions

This next strategy is almost like cheating because it's so effective yet so easy. All you have to do is sit back in your favorite chair or lie down in bed and put on some headphones.

What you're playing through those headphones is the secret.

I personally have several songs that, when I listen to them, give me a boost of energy and encourage me to exercise or at least help me charge my body with oxygen through some rapid deep breathing. Other songs remind me of a happy moment or inspire me to sing out loud. All of these reactions create positive reactions in the body and reduce stress levels.

More advanced headphone sessions involve listening to self-hypnosis tracks. There are many specific ones to choose from: everything from stress relief, to overcoming guilt, stopping smoking, stopping nail biting—you can probably find a self-hypnosis track tailored to your need. Self-hypnosis is not only incredibly relaxing, but it trains our subconscious mind to be in alignment with our desires. Remember, the subconscious is very, very powerful.

For further information about self-hypnosis, go to CraigBrockie.com/Feeling for some recommended courses that will have an immediate impact on your life.

Brain wave entrainment audio programs are also outstanding and are one of the most powerful ways to take you out of the "my-mind-just-won't-stop-thinking" beta brainwave state into the various other levels of consciousness. You can achieve meditative states deeper than a Zen monk with some of these audio tracks.

Do What You Love

Another idea is to schedule time to be in the moment doing whatever it is you love.

Turn off your cell phone to avoid distractions and have fun. When we were children, all we did was play. Most adults have forgotten how joyful life can be when we stop taking ourselves so seriously. Some of the best advice I've ever received was to follow my children's lead when it comes to having fun. Playing with children is a great learning experience both for the children and adults.

Exercise

Exercising also boosts our energy levels and mood. Exercising should never seem like a chore and any exercise is better than none. I hope that after trying some of the suggestions so far you feel more motivated and passionate about life and will adopt a sport or hobby that keeps being active fun for you.

Be Happy Every Day

There are many other simple and straightforward techniques you can use to reduce stress and feel happier in your everyday life. Here are some examples:

- Focus your attention on a happy memory and relive the moment in your mind.

- Adopt an attitude of gratitude. If you can afford to buy this book, you're more fortunate than the majority of people on this planet. Make a list of all the things you're thankful for and keep it with you. I've got my list on my iPhone for easy reference whenever I'm feeling down.

- Write a heartfelt letter to someone you love, appreciate, or admire. Not only will you be making the day of the person receiving the letter, you will likely be making their month or at least their week. I also find that while it feels good to write the letter, the positive feedback I receive from the recipient is priceless.

- Decide if you are a perfectionist or an imperfectionist. A person who is never satisfied and focuses on imperfection considers themselves a perfectionist. I fell into this category until I had an epiphany in an ayahuasca ceremony. What I learned was that although I considered myself a perfectionist, in reality I was an imperfectionist. A perfectionist is really someone who is focused on what's perfect in the world and what's going on around them. There really are far more good things than bad, more kind people than evil ones, and more love than hate in this world. I now choose to focus my attention on what's good about things and highly recommend you do too.

- Focus your attention on making the people around you feel good about themselves. The good vibrations are contagious and come back to you amplified. Besides showing your appreciation for others, another great strategy to use is the three-part compliment. Have you ever given someone a compliment only to have it bounced back to you, dismissed, or perhaps even questioned for its sincerity or intent? Using the three-part compliment, you're guaranteed to have your compliments sincerely accepted and appreciated every time. You'll find a short demonstration video for the three-part compliment on my web site.

- Make eye contact and smile at strangers. Although some people don't smile back, those that do make up for all those who do not, and then some.

- Read *How to Work a Room* by Susan Roane (Harper Paperbacks, 2007) and Dale Carnegie's *How to Win Friends and Influence People* (Pocket, 1998) for more strategies to raise your confidence in social situations and for advice about turning strangers into friends. Most people feel shy and hate being the first to introduce themselves or even say hello. By gaining the know-how and confidence to turn strangers into friends, life becomes much more exciting and fun.

Now You've Improved How You Feel...

Once you've implemented some of the suggestions in this chapter, your outlook on life is likely to improve, your stress levels will be lower and you'll be feeling happier. I hope that by this point, your need for coffee will have diminished. If not, consider doing some research into replacing coffee with green tea, yerba mate tea, or the herb ephedra for a few weeks, just to get you over the hump while we super-charge your body.

You're not alone in feeling some level of insecurity, sadness, or worry—these emotions have become the norm in our society. As you become happier and calmer, be sure to "pay it forward" by sharing what you find effective with others. I encourage you to share information in a playful, "hey check this out" kind of way, rather than preaching. Those who are open to change are the best students and will be attracted to you. Teaching is the best way to master the art of wellness.

Chapter 3
Flood Your Body with Oxygen

The oxygen in the air we breathe is arguably our most important resource, yet most of us take it for granted. We can last for weeks without food, days without water, but only minutes without air. Take a deep breath and hold it. How long can you make it without breathing?

Oxygen is fundamental not only to our survival, but also to the health of our environment and planet as a whole. I recall an episode of *The Nature of Things* hosted by world famous scientist David Suzuki where he explained how our rivers and streams detoxify by oxygen in the air being drawn into the water in areas of turbulence such as white water or even gentle "burbling" over rocks. And surely you know that our planet is surrounded by a protective ozone layer. Ozone is simply O_3, an active form of oxygen. Step outside after a lightning storm and you'll smell the fresh scent of ozone in the air.

Not only does nature survive and thrive with oxygen, but so do our bodies. In fact, flooding our bodies with oxygen is one of the fastest and most effective ways I know of to recover from illness. Oxygen therapies have been used for over 100 years. Beyond that, they are affordable and have a proven track record for safely and routinely reversing even the most dire of terminal illnesses including AIDS and late-stage cancer. Oxygen therapies are commonly used in Germany, Russia, Italy, and Cuba as well as naturopathic clinics in North America.

Naturopathic medicine expert Dr. Lorne Swetlikoff states that intravenous hydrogen peroxide therapy and blood ozone treatments are the most effective methods of treating infectious diseases and keeping our families safe throughout a pandemic. We'll look at some of these therapies later in this chapter.

Hollywood star Nick Nolte is featured in the informative documentary *Ozone: A Medical Breakthrough*, explaining how he uses ozone treatments to avoid getting (herpes) cold sores brought on by nervous tension.

Best-selling author Ed McCabe is a leading authority in the field of oxygen therapies. His book, *Flood Your Body with Oxygen* (Breath Of God Ministry,

2004) is in my opinion a must-read for anyone serious about mastering the art of wellness.

This chapter gives a brief overview of the work of McCabe and other medical oxygen experts.

Oxygen Starvation

Have you ever been held under water against your will? If so, the chances are you didn't enjoy the experience. In fact, you probably experienced panic. You may have screamed or even resorted to punching and kicking to get yourself out of the situation. Desperate times call for desperate measures.

Not only do we need oxygen to survive, but so does every cell in our body. If a cell is deprived of oxygen, it too will resort to desperate measures in order to survive. When cells are chronically starved of oxygen, the natural oxidative metabolic process is unable to function properly. Rather than just give up and die, our cells put up a fight by adapting solely to a glucose fermentation metabolic process—in other words, they create energy exclusively from glucose, rather than from oxygen—and self-replicate uncontrollably. We call this cancer.

If you or a loved one has cancer, you may be relieved to know that cancer cannot survive in an oxygen-rich environment. Nobel Prize winner Otto Warburg proved this to be true. McCabe's book provides page after page further substantiating this fact and

I know several people who have overcome cancer using oxygen therapies. Rather than devastating the body with chemotherapy or radiation therapy, why not do a little due diligence into oxygen therapies? You do have alternatives.

If you've been feeling run down lately, you might find it interesting to understand the direct relationship between oxygen and energy. You probably already know that the main reason we yawn when we are tired is to draw more oxygen into our bodies. It should come as no surprise then that highly oxygenated cells carry a much higher voltage than cells deficient in oxygen. Flooding our bodies with oxygen is therefore a great way to boost and maintain high energy levels.

Now let's talk about "incurable" diseases such as AIDS as well as disease in general. All harmful bacteria, viruses, and parasites are anaerobic which means they cannot survive in oxygen. One study which demonstrates this fact involved injecting monkeys with blood plasma infected with a deadly strain of Simian Immunodeficiency Virus (the monkey equivalent of HIV). The first group of monkeys all died within 12 days. The second group's infected plasma was infused with ozone prior to injection. None of the monkeys in the second group showed any signs of infection.

Take a moment to consider the implications for

humanity that a cure for HIV/AIDS would have.

You might be thinking "OK Craig, that was a study with monkeys, not humans." Added to which the oxygenation occurred outside the body prior to injection, not in the body after the virus had already been acquired.

And you are right to be questioning. Fortunately, there are thousands of former HIV and AIDS patients around the world who have eliminated their symptoms and have come back with lab reports showing the virus undetectable, all thanks to oxygen therapies. Some patients in Africa have reportedly achieved these results spending just pennies a day.

If you're not suffering from terminal AIDS or cancer, you'll be pleased to know that oxygen therapies benefit most people, regardless of their ailment.

Am I stating that oxygen therapies are a cure-all? Yes and no. I believe increasing the cellular oxygen levels throughout our bodies creates an unwelcome environment for pain and disease to exist. I also believe that there are a few more pieces to the puzzle to ensure the body can absorb and retain optimal levels of oxygen, which we will review in later chapters.

So why hasn't the public been educated about oxygen therapies? I believe the answer is threefold:

1. Oxygen therapies are safe and effective.

2. Oxygen therapies are affordable.

3. Oxygen therapies cannot be patented.

Pharmaceutical companies spend billions of dollars each year lobbying, employing former regulatory executives, financially supporting medical schools, and advertising to doctors' consumers (the patients). Is it a conspiracy? In my opinion no, it's just business. Unfortunately, profits come before people and oxygen therapies are a threat to the bottom line. I choose to avoid taking the health care system personally or judging the situation. I just accept it for what it is, and focus my attention on solutions.

Alright, we've set the table, outlining what oxygen therapies are capable of, and we've spiced things up by discussing why you might not have heard of them. Now let's get to the meat of the issue and how you can take control of your health by flooding your body with oxygen.

Breathe Deeply

Breathing is something most of us take for granted. Unless you have asthma or are into yoga, qigong, or some form of meditation, you probably don't give breathing much thought. Most people are shallow breathers and absorb only a fraction of their potential oxygen as a result. If you'd like to increase your lung capacity and the oxygen you absorb, practice this simple breathing exercise:

1. Inhale through your nose, expanding your stomach first and your chest second. Most people only expand their chest, so this may feel strange to begin with.

2. Once you've taken in what normally would seem like a full breath, pause and take three more sips of air to further expand your lung capacity and gently stretch the tight muscles in your abdomen and chest that restrict your breathing capacity.

3. Now hold the breath for a three count, relaxing into the experience.

4. Exhale, contracting your chest first and your stomach second.

5. At the end of your exhale, really squeeze your abdominal muscles to get as much stale air out of your lungs as possible.

6. Repeat several times and enjoy the buzz.

I encourage you to practice this breathing exercise before getting out of bed in the morning, before falling asleep at night, and anytime throughout the day when you're feeling bored, stressed, or tired.

Once you've got the technique down, try adding these simple suggestions to further enhance your experience and the benefits:

- Experience a super-charged endorphin release by listening to some of your favorite music, keeping a smile on your face, and/or focusing your mind on a happy memory.

- Super-expand your breathing capacity by getting a deep tissue massage on your abdomen and chest.

  Most people prefer having their backs massaged since this is where they carry pain. By focusing more attention on loosening the muscles in the front of your torso, you will be able to take much deeper breaths, allowing more oxygen into your body. This type of massage can also improve internal organ function and will likely improve your posture, helping you stand taller.

  A simple and less expensive technique to loosen up the muscles of the abdomen, chest, and pelvis is to take a basketball or volleyball and lie face down on the floor or an exercise mat. Lie on the ball and gently ease your body weight into the ball. As you relax and exhale, the ball will sink deeper into your body, releasing many of the tight muscles which are restricting your breathing. You can find a free video demonstration of this ball massage technique at CraigBrockie.com/Oxygen so you can see how this technique works in practice.

- If you can afford to do so, you might consider investing in an oxygen tank or oxygen concentrator to allow you to breathe pure oxygen during your breathing exercises and even while you sleep. You might also consider exercising with oxygen therapy (EWOT) as a relatively affordable method to flood your body with oxygen. If you play sports, you'll realize a noticeable improvement in your performance simply by breathing oxygen for 10-20 minutes before you play.

Oxygen tanks are less than $200 and can be refilled for less than $30—many people spend more money on their morning lattes. For convenience, I bought several small oxygen tanks and have a large oxygen tank with a transfill adapter to refill the smaller tanks.

Oxygen Supplements

Now that we've addressed how to maximize our breathing capacity and increase our oxygen absorption through our lungs, let's look at other affordable and effective ways to get more oxygen into our system.

The air we breathe is at best 20% oxygen and far less in urban areas. McCabe cites a study where the oxygen content in the air in Gary, Indiana was measured at less than 12%! Whether you live in an urban area or not, oxygen supplementation is something you may benefit from to super-charge your health and energy levels.

Before we look at the oxygen supplements, a quick warning: If at any time during your oxygen supplementation process your symptoms get worse, this is a sign that you are oxidizing microbes and toxins faster than your body is eliminating them. If this is the case, reduce your dosage level slightly and put more emphasis on the elimination strategies covered in chapter 1.

Hydrogen Peroxide

The least expensive form of oxygen supplementation is to consume drops of food grade hydrogen peroxide in drinking water. McCabe shares many documented cases of impoverished African patients curing themselves of AIDS using this method alone—all at a cost of just pennies a day. Hydrogen peroxide has not only demonstrated its ability to cure AIDS, but can be effective in treating most other diseases as well, including cancer and heart disease.

The most recognizable form of hydrogen peroxide is the product you find in most grocery stores and pharmacies. If you've ever used this product, you know how it creates a white fizzy reaction when applied to an open cut or a scrape to the skin. This fizzing action sanitizes the wound through a process called oxidation, which I'll explain in a moment.

Before we get ahead of ourselves, let's take a look at what hydrogen peroxide actually is. I'm sure you've heard water referred to as H_2O before, right? Well hydrogen peroxide is simply H_2O_2: a water molecule which is eager to donate the electrons from its extra oxygen atom.

Water is a much more stable substance than hydrogen peroxide, therefore hydrogen peroxide donates its extra oxygen to anything that will react with it. This reaction is called oxidation and it sanitizes the inside of the body as effectively as it does the outside. The great news is that all harmful bacteria, viruses, and parasites that plague humanity are anaerobic and are killed on contact with oxygen! This is the reason why flooding the body with oxygen is so effective.

If the miraculous healing ability of hydrogen peroxide is news to you, don't worry, your body has always known. As a matter of fact, hydrogen peroxide is produced by our white blood cells as our front line defense against harmful pathogens. That's right; our immune system produces hydrogen peroxide as our first line of defense, which is why licensed naturopathic doctors will often give their patients intravenous treatments containing hydrogen peroxide to help the immune system combat disease.

I hope you're getting a sense of how outstanding hydrogen peroxide is for healing the body. A convincing test I encourage you to try at home is to add half a cap full of (3% strength) hydrogen peroxide into your mouth—in addition to your favorite toothpaste—next time you brush your teeth. You'll be absolutely amazed at how much cleaner your teeth feel after just one application. I use hydrogen peroxide every time I brush and floss my teeth and my dentist is always amazed how clean my teeth are and how healthy my gums are when I come in for a visit every couple of years.

You should note that most hydrogen peroxide is labeled for external use only due to added chemical stabilizers, but for a one-off test, I assure you that you've put far worse things in your mouth. Although you spit out the hydrogen peroxide after brushing, I recommend using a diluted form of food grade hydrogen peroxide for everyday dental hygiene. There is a video on my web site demonstrating how to dilute food grade hydrogen peroxide for this use.

Getting back to oxygen supplementation, adding drops of hydrogen peroxide to our drinking water is hands-down the least expensive way to go and we know it works. I've already mentioned how AIDS patients in Africa have cured themselves with hydrogen peroxide. McCabe also cites examples in his book of farmers who buy diseased livestock and return them to perfect health simply by adding hydrogen peroxide to their water supply.

For long-term or regular use, to avoid ingesting the heavy metals and toxic stabilizers found in standard store-bought hydrogen peroxide, only food grade hydrogen peroxide should be used for internal use. Food grade hydrogen peroxide can be found in most health food stores and hydroponic gardening outlets. Food grade hydrogen peroxide is over 10-times stronger than the standard hydrogen peroxide and so needs to be handled with care.

A safe and effective protocol for taking hydrogen peroxide internally can be found in McCabe's book.

Stabilized Oxygen Supplements

Although hydrogen peroxide can provide miraculous results when taken orally in a consistent and progressive manner, you may not appreciate the chalky taste or the bleaching effect that 35% strength H_2O_2 can have on your clothes and fingers if mishandled.

Fortunately, there are many stabilized liquid oxygen supplements on the market today. Many of these products have a more pleasant taste and provide similar benefits to taking hydrogen peroxide orally. I've tested about a dozen of these products and continue to try new ones. You can find my personal favorites at CraigBrockie.com/Oxygen along with other oxygen-related resources.

Other excellent oxygen supplements are oxygenating colon cleaners. I made reference to *OxyFlush* in chapter 1 as an alternative you could consider to using herbal laxative tea. In that chapter I discussed how important regular elimination and colon health is—oxygenating colon cleaners have the dual benefit of stimulating regular elimination and also releasing active oxygen into the colon. This oxygenating action:

- kills harmful bacterial, viruses, and parasites in the colon
- helps the colon heal, and
- releases excess oxygen throughout the body.

Topical Oxygen Supplements

So far we've talked about flooding our bodies with oxygen from the inside out, which is the best way to go when dealing with the body as a whole. That said, many people suffer from local skin conditions such as acne, eczema, psoriasis, athlete's foot, ringworm, and herpes, to name a few.

When it comes to skin conditions, topical oxygen supplements provide absolutely amazing results. For instance, those who suffer from shaving irritation or acne can benefit from misting the skin with 3% hydrogen peroxide from a spray bottle. In addition, ozonated olive oil provides outstanding results for most infections, including stubborn issues such as athlete's foot, jock itch, and ringworm. (Since these later conditions are all fungus related, a Candida cleanse is also important.)

Anyone who suffers from cold sores or any other herpes condition will benefit immensely from reading the book, *Never an Outbreak* (Printo Publishing, 2005) by William Fharel, which explains how topical application of DMSO (dimethyl sulfoxide) cream can be used to eliminate all further outbreaks. DMSO also provides penetrating relief to sore muscles and joints.

Medical Oxygen Therapies

If you to prefer to keep your budget to a minimum and you have the wonderful quality called patience, then the suggestions already mentioned in this chapter are likely to satisfy your needs.

If, on the other hand, you are terminally ill and/or have the resources to fast-track the optimization of your health, I suggest exploring some of the following medical oxygen therapies.

Hyperbaric Oxygen Therapy

Hyperbaric Oxygen Therapy (HBOT) is definitely the most mainstream of the medical oxygen therapies, largely because of the attention generated by professional sports. Professional athletes frequently use HBOT to speed their recovery from injury. HBOT has also gained attention as a successful treatment for children with autism.

HBOT is effective in flooding the body with oxygen because the hyperbaric chamber pressurizes the body while the patient simultaneously breathes pure oxygen. The pressurization allows far more oxygen to saturate the cells of the body than is the case when we simply breathe oxygen at atmospheric pressure.

An everyday example to understand the pressurization effect is illustrated when we open a can of soda. As soon as we open the can, excess carbon dioxide is released. The release of carbon dioxide from an opened can of soda provides evidence that the concentration of the gas was much higher when the can remained under pressure. Therefore, by first pressurizing the body, far more oxygen is able to be absorbed.

Hyperbaric oxygen chambers are found in most major cities. Sessions usually last an hour and cost about $100 per treatment. Portable hyperbaric chambers for the home are also now available.

Intravenous Hydrogen Peroxide

As mentioned earlier in this chapter, medical grade hydrogen peroxide can be taken intravenously under the care of a licensed naturopathic doctor. Our white blood cells naturally produce hydrogen peroxide to kill pathogens, which is why this method of oxygenation is so effective in assisting the body to overcome disease. Intravenous hydrogen peroxide treatment takes less than an hour and costs about $100.

Ozone Cupping, Bagging, and Steam Cabinets

Ozone cupping involves covering a small area of the body with a direct flow of ozone. Ozone bagging involves enclosing an area of the body with a bag and saturating the area with ozone. Ozone cupping and bagging help facilitate rapid healing for skin conditions such as infections and burns.

Saunas and steam rooms have been used for centuries to provide detoxification through the body's largest organ, the skin. Ozone Steam Cabinets provide all the benefits of a regular steam treatment, plus the additional benefit of saturating the skin with healing ozone. Ozone steam cabinets are available in many major cities and can be purchased for the home. Ozone steam cabinets are shaped like a clam shell in which you sit. The cabinet closes around your neck, which is comfortably wrapped in a towel to lock in the steam heat while allowing the user to breath the air outside of the cabinet. Most practitioners use a white towel for the user to sit on while in the cabinet—this readily shows the dark toxins that have exited the body.

Ozone Insufflation

Ozone treatments can be effective when administered:

- rectally

- vaginally, and

- through the ear canal.

Dual catheter rectal ozone insufflation, in my opinion, is excellent for anyone dealing with colon, prostate, reproductive, or liver disorders, as well as sexually transmitted diseases (STDs). Vaginal insufflation is known to be a very effective remedy for yeast infections, STDs, and reproductive health conditions. Ear and sinus infections can be effectively cleared with the gentle application of ozone gas into the ear canal.

Ozone insufflation is not only a great treatment for local symptoms, but also provides increased oxygen throughout the rest of body. For example, similar to the effect oxygenating colon cleansers, ozone administered rectally is absorbed into the blood through the walls of the colon. Ozone administered vaginally or through the ear also results in increased oxygenation levels throughout the body.

Probably the best benefit of ozone insufflation is that it can safely and affordably be administered in the convenience of your own home by investing in a medical ozone generator and oxygen tank.

Ozone Autohemotherapy

In Germany, ozone has played an important role in

the nation's healthcare system for decades. German practitioners are the world's leading authorities in a medical ozone procedure called autohemotherapy (AHT). North America's leading authority in the field of AHT is Dr. Frank Shallenberger.

AHT involves treating up to 500ml of blood outside the body with ozone. AHT is convincing treatment for even the greatest of skeptics as you can see the effects right before your eyes. As the blood leaves the body, it is dark purple, brown, or even black. The darker the blood, the worse the patient's current health status.

After the blood has been collected in a clear sterile container, ozone gas is injected. Immediately the blood turns a bright cherry red color as it is teeming with oxygen, energy, and life. Right before your eyes you see blood being super-charged with oxygen!

Even though you may be treating less than 10% of your total blood volume at a time, AHT provides an excellent health boost. In addition to the oxygen boost, as ozone kills the harmful microbes present in your blood, it creates natural antibodies specific to your condition. As the oxygenated blood is returned to the body, the immune system gets a boost from both the oxygen and the cascading effect of the antibodies.

AHT is relatively painless and is available through licensed naturopathic doctors in most major cities.

It usually costs about $125 per treatment.

Direct Intravenous Ozone Injection

The most controversial method to flood the body with oxygen is to administer ozone by direct intravenous (IV) injection. Direct intravenous ozone injection has been safely used by many terminal cancer and AIDS patients to rapidly overturn their death sentences. Once a person has the required equipment and training, a treatment can be administered from the comfort of one's home.

There is a lot of controversy and fear surrounding direct intravenous ozone administration. The fear is that injecting ozone gas directly into a vein will create an embolism. An embolism is a gas bubble in the blood and can be fatal. There's nothing like scaring a person about probable death to make them overlook an affordable miracle cure!!

The controversy and fear of direct intravenous ozone is based on a truth, but coupled with an incomplete understanding. If a person were to inject ozone gas generated from ambient air as the source gas, then there is risk of an embolism. This is because air is 80% nitrogen and nitrogen is insoluble in the blood, which could lead to an embolism.

However, medical grade ozone is made from pure oxygen gas, not ambient air. Medical grade ozone is therefore completely soluble and hence eliminates the risk of an embolism. This means that the ozone can be absorbed into the blood immediately on injection.

McCabe has interviewed enough doctors and patients to represent thousands of direct intravenous ozone injections with a safety record the conventional medical system could never dream of achieving. This method is safe when a person is properly trained, proper equipment is used, and the administration protocol is followed with care.

EBOO Ozone Treatments

EBOO or Extracorporeal Blood Oxygenation and Ozonation is a blood filtration process which is combined with the introduction of high doses of ozone. If I became terminally ill with AIDS or Hepatitis C, I would do whatever possible to receive a series of EBOO treatments. EBOO is closest thing to getting brand new blood.

Dark purple, brown, or even black (diseased) blood is drawn from the body and infused with active oxygen, which instantly turns the blood a bright cherry red color while also killing all anaerobic bacteria, viruses, and parasites. The blood is then filtered and safely returned to the body, all in a closed loop system similar to dialysis. The sterile, super-charged, cherry red blood then circulates throughout the body facilitating a rapid rate of healing. Used in conjunction with improved nutrition, EBOO may be the most effective protocol for overcoming any disease, terminal or otherwise, but is also one of the more expensive, starting at $1,250 per treatment (requiring several treatments).

I love this treatment—it's like having your blood changed in 90 minutes.

EBOO can also be undertaken in conjunction with intravenous nutrients. When your gut is coated with mucus and Candida, your nutrient absorption can be quite limited, so even if you orally consume high doses of nutrients and vitamins, their effect can be low. Intravenous vitamins and nutrients are vital for terminal cases because they get the nutrition into the body quickly and directly.

Other Ozone Therapies

Lesser-known medical ozone applications also yield similar amazing results. One such protocol is to inject highly concentrated ozone gas directly into cancerous tumors. According to Dr. Turska (who was a naturopathic doctor and also appointed chairman of the board of trustees of the national medical society) in this case the ozone destroys the diseased tissue at a rapid rate.

Another unique ozone application is particularly hopeful for anyone suffering from back pain, especially those with herniated disks. The procedure claims a 95% success rate with no side effects and zero recovery time. Developed in Italy, The Discosan Method is now available at advanced clinics worldwide.

Getting More Oxygen Every Day

Before we move on to the next chapter, I would like to introduce to you some final ideas to consider adding to your home to flood your body with oxygen.

Violet Ray

A handheld device known as a violet ray can be effective for pain relief, countering the effects of hair loss, and helping to rapidly heal many local health conditions. The violet ray device topically transfers ozone and electrical stimulation to the area being treated, increasing oxygen levels, blood flow, and healing energy. The "father of holistic medicine," Edgar Cayce, used the violet ray extensively with his patients due to the device's effectiveness.

Oxygenated Water Cooler

If you're not into adding drops to your drinking water and you have the floor space available, you might consider getting an oxygenating water cooler. If you don't want to have a water cooler sitting in your kitchen, then an under-the-counter water ionizer is perhaps a better option. I discuss this in the next chapter.

Improving Indoor Air Quality

The quality of indoor air is a major issue these days, especially at times of the year when exterior windows are kept closed to maintain the temperature inside, whether heating during winter or air conditioning during summer. There are many irritants that circulate within indoor air, including:

- mold spores
- airborne bacteria
- viruses, and
- synthetic toxins such as formaldehyde from carpets.

Introducing an ozone generator to a building's central heating or ventilation system is an excellent option to consider. Ozone kills mold spores, viruses, and bacteria, and oxidizes toxins, rendering them less harmful to the body. Ozone also leaves the air smelling much fresher by eliminating most odors, including those from dampness, garbage, pets, and even cigarette smoke.

Ozone in high concentrations can be irritating to the lungs, so low levels of ozone are always used in interior spaces. The rule of thumb is that concentrations should be low enough that the smell of ozone is absent when occupied. We have an ozone generator installed in the central ventilation system for our home and really enjoy the benefits. Higher concentrations of ozone can be used to kill off mold or eliminate heavy odors, but only when spaces are unoccupied.

In our home we also have a medical ozone generator along with pure oxygen source gas and all the accessories needed to perform many of the ozone protocols mentioned in this chapter. For about $2,000 you too can have a lifetime of medical ozone in the convenience of your own home.

Getting More Oxygen

Many people will ask whether ozone treatments are safe. The German Medical Society has reported that 384,775 patients were given 5,579,238 applications of ozone with a side effect rate of 0.0005%.

But ozone isn't the only way to get oxygen into our bodies. Medical ozone expert, Dr. Louie Yu (North America's leading authority on EBOO) states that deep breathing is the best way to keep the body in a high oxygen state. You can boost your health by following the simple breathing exercise outlined in this chapter and by focusing more attention on breathing more deeply at all times.

Oxygen supplementation is as simple and affordable as adding food grade hydrogen peroxide or stabilized oxygen drops to drinking water. This can also be effective in increasing cellular oxygen levels throughout the body. Those with the resources available will also find the medical oxygen therapies mentioned in this chapter very helpful.

In years to come, as oxygen treatments are used more widely, cancer and AIDS may be seen in the same way as we see scurvy today, in other words, as obsolete diseases.

Visit CraigBrockie.com/Oxygen where you can find more information and links to many of the oxygen therapies and products mentioned in this chapter.

Now go and flood your body with oxygen and enjoy the amazing benefits! Then check out the next chapter, which looks at acid-related issues and identifies ways to maintain a pH-balanced lifestyle.

Chapter 4
Acidosis: Putting Out the Fire

Imagine for a moment that a raging forest fire is threatening your home. You'd have good reason to be concerned, don't you think? Most people understand the devastation a fire can cause.

Now consider for a moment that you could have a fire raging inside your own body. While this fire is a bit different, anyone who recalls high school chemistry can understand it. The blazing fire inside the body is called acidosis. In many ways, acidosis is a silent killer.

If high school is a distant memory to you, perhaps a torture scene from a Hollywood movie has sensationalized the corrosive, burning effects of acid on a victim's skin. Or if you've ever replaced a car battery, you might have noticed the warning labels about avoiding contact with the battery acid inside. There's no arguing that acid is able to burn human tissue.

However, like anything, acid is neither good nor bad in absolute terms. In fact, stomach acid is essential to facilitate proper digestion. But, while our stomachs thrive in a highly acidic environment, the same cannot be said for all areas of the body. For instance, if our blood becomes too acidic, we die.

pH

Before we continue, we need to talk a bit about pH or potential hydrogen as it is sometimes called. The pH scale ranges from 0 to 14 with seven being neutral. An acid is any substance with a pH less than seven. Any substance with a pH greater than seven is an alkali.

An interesting characteristic of the pH scale is that it is logarithmic, with every point representing a change by a factor of 10. Therefore a one point change equals 10-times, a two point change equals 100-times, a three point change equals 1,000-times, and so on. To illustrate, distilled water has a neutral pH of seven while many carbonated soft drinks have a pH of less than four. Sodas may therefore be least 1,000 times more acidic than distilled water.

pH and Oxygen

In the last chapter we discussed the importance of oxygen to our health. Interestingly, there is a direct relationship between pH and oxygen. Acidic environments are:

- deficient in available oxygen
- susceptible to disease, and
- unsupportive of life.

By contrast, alkaline environments are:

- rich in available oxygen
- resistant to disease, and
- supportive of life.

A real-world example may help illustrate how acids affect an environment. Acid rain was a hot topic in the 1980s. The problem was so severe in some places that acid was overwhelming entire lakes, lowering the pH of the water to the point that it could no longer support life. These acidic lakes were eventually categorized as dead.

Oxygen doesn't disappear in an acidic environment; instead acids bind to the oxygen, making it unavailable for other purposes. The remedy for dead lakes was to add alkaline mineral—usually lime—to the water. Lime increases the alkalinity of the water, which increased the amount of available oxygen in the water. The lime-treated lakes would then begin coming back to life, and be capable of supporting and sustaining the plants and fish that had previously lived in the lake.

Another real-world example to help understand the importance of pH is familiar to anyone who owns a swimming pool or hot tub. Although they may not understand why, hot tub owners know it is important to keep the pH of the water slightly alkaline. A pH of 7.2 to 7.6 is the target range to keep hot tubbers safe and healthy.

Acidosis

Most areas of the body—for instance, our blood—thrive in an environment that is slightly alkaline. Our bodies function in a very narrow pH range, for instance, our blood is allowed to fluctuate from 7.35 to 7.45. Unfortunately, most of the things we eat, drink and do in a day create an abundance of acid.

Virtually all of the toxins that build up in the body are acidic. Acidic toxins can prevent our bodies from absorbing the nutrients from our food and supplements that our cells require. Toxic wastes keep our bodies in an acidic, low oxygen state that encourages the breeding of fungus, mold, bacteria, and viruses, thus making us susceptible to disease

Acidosis is the condition associated with having an increased level of acidity in the body. There are numerous symptoms of acidosis and they can affect many areas of the body. The symptoms include:

- lack of energy and sleepiness; this lack of energy may even manifest as chronic fatigue
- overweight, or sometimes, ironically, underweight
- joint pain and arthritis
- osteoporosis
- heart attack
- allergies
- acne, and
- frequent colds, bronchitis, infections, and headaches.

Reducing Acid in the Body

So if we're agreed that excess acid (and acidosis) can have detrimental effects on the body, what can we do about it?

In the same way that a forest fire consumes oxygen to support its combustion process, an acidic body consumes oxygen to create acidic carbon dioxide. Following the analogy, the answer is not to simply throw more oxygen at the issue—although that is one course—but to try to put out the fire, by finding what caused it in the first place.

As a result, there is no single treatment, but instead a range of options that can be incorporated into daily life.

Reduce Stress

A first step to putting out that fire is to reduce stress. Among other things, stress can lead to:

- Shallow breathing, which results in insufficient oxygen absorption.
- A fight-or-flight chemical response, which is acidic.
- Muscle tension, which is also acid-forming.

I'll elaborate on this issue in the next chapter, but you should also be aware that there is a relationship between Candida and stress, since excess Candida in the body creates a biochemical imbalance that adds to stress.

Breathe Deeply

Our prime source of oxygen comes through breathing. As you will have read in the last chapter, many people do not gain the full benefit of the oxygen that is in the air due to their shallow breathing and so are missing out on the opportunity to increase the oxygen in their system in the most natural way.

Check back to the last chapter for advice about

breathing exercises as these are a great way to increase oxygen in the body.

Alkaline Water

In the last chapter we discussed how cellular oxygen levels can be increased by drinking water enriched with oxygen. While an oxygen water cooler can be purchased for the home, it is important to know that oxygen saturation only works with cold, not hot water. It's also important to know that the excess oxygen dissipates quickly from an open glass of water and is entirely gone within 30 minutes. Carrying water in a smaller, sealed water bottle is one solution, but may not be appropriate in your home environment.

An oxygen water cooler also consumes precious space in your kitchen. For about the same price, an alkaline water ionizer can be purchased. Water ionizers filter and process regular tap water into health-enhancing water. Ionizers can raise the pH of regular tap water from seven to over 10, making the water up to 1,000 times more alkaline than "regular" water. Drinking alkaline water is an excellent way to raise the pH of the body and since oxygen availability and pH are so closely related, focusing on raising one's pH also helps flood the body with oxygen. The water ionizer model I use in my home is mounted under the counter, which I highly recommend to save counter space around your sink.

Water ionizers have another benefit in that they greatly enhance the oxidation reduction potential (ORP) of the water. I won't go into a lot of detail here about ORP as it is a somewhat complex topic, but I will simply mention that the "dreaded" free radicals that get so much attention these days are electron deficient and water ionizers generate water rich in negative ions. The excess negative ions in the water are understood to be very effective in neutralizing free radicals within the body.

Alkalizing Diet

Besides the water we drink, the other things we put in our bodies also affect our pH. Soda, as I mentioned earlier, is extremely acidic and the standard American diet is so dominated by acid foods that it is no wonder Americans are statistically so unhealthy. Coffee, alcohol, sugar, bread, dairy, and meat are all acid-forming. Alakali forming foods are primarily fruits, vegetables, and most seeds/nuts. If you go to CraigBrockie.com/Alkalize you can find a chart of acid and alkali forming foods.

It is recommended that we consume more alkaline foods than acid foods as a percentage of our diets. That said, changing one's diet can be one of the greatest challenges any person undertakes. Rather than trying to make drastic changes, I suggest gradually putting more emphasis on alkaline foods and less on acidic foods. As your body becomes healthier you'll find that you crave "junk" foods less and healthy foods more.

Minerals

In the agricultural belt of the US, soil depletion is a big issue. It is widely accepted that as a result of over-farming, the soil in which the crops that feed the nation are grown is deficient in minerals. Instead of taking action to replenish the natural minerals that have been lost from the soil, the agricultural industry has instead chosen to use chemical fertilizers and pesticides to increase their crop yield. While this increases crops, the quality of those crops is degraded—if the soil doesn't have minerals, then the crops don't have minerals. Plants can create vitamins as part of the photosynthesis process, but they cannot generate minerals.

The end result is that the mineral content of the US food supply has dropped. This is a particular challenge since minerals are alkaline. When you couple the effect acidosis robbing the body of alkalis with the depletion of alkaline minerals entering the body through the food chain, you can see that the body's pH levels can become increasingly acidic.

There are different forms of minerals, most commonly found in tablets and capsules. On the whole, these are the lowest quality supplements in terms of bioavailability to the body. Colloidal minerals are an improvement, but the best form of mineral supplementation are liquid ionic minerals which are significantly easier to absorb into the system. These include trace minerals, which help maintain the natural balance.

The two most common minerals are:

- Calcium, which has a tightening effect inside the body, helping to make bones denser, as one example of a benefit. Calcium supplements can often help in connection with osteoporosis (the condition which arises when calcium is robbed from the bones).

- Magnesium, which has a loosening effect on the body, helping the muscles relax. It also relaxes the stomach and has a relaxing effect for those who suffer from anxiety.

Bicarbonate

There are alkaline substances and there are acidic substances. Then there are buffer levels in a liquid.

This may be illustrated by looking at a swimming pool. When we measure the pool levels, we don't just measure the pH value, we also measure the total alkalinity. Total alkalinity refers to how much bicarbonate is in the water, and the more bicarbonate there is in the water, the more resistant the water is to spikes in pH. With greater bicarbonate levels the water will not be so readily affected by the addition of acid. In essence, the bicarbonate has the effect of a stabilizer.

Bicarbonate levels in the body perform a similar function and can help to stabilize the pH. Bicarbonate can be taken orally, but for terminal cancer cases, bicarbonate is often administered intravenously to rapidly alkalize the body.

An Alkaline Life

The process to introduce more alkalis into our bodies is a comparatively straightforward and requires little in the way of lifestyle change. However, the benefits are huge and begin immediately, and not only that, they will improve our health in many different ways and strengthen our systems from within.

Once we are on the road to improving our internal systems, we can think about getting rid of the trash that's there at the moment. The next chapter looks at how we can take out the trash and get rid of those unwanted toxins that wash around inside our bodies.

Chapter 5
Taking Out the Trash: Bacteria, Virus, and Parasite Elimination

We have looked at toxins and how to rinse away some of the most toxic substances which reside in the colon. We have begun increasing the oxygenation and pH inside the body, thereby creating an environment where anaerobic viruses, bacteria, and parasites cannot exist. In this chapter we will cover how to rid ourselves of toxins that have settled throughout the rest of the body.

As I write this chapter, there is concern about a global flu pandemic. The good news is that by taking control of your health you will be bolstering your immunity to all disease, including all forms of the flu virus and any new mutations of the virus that have yet to occur. To give you even greater comfort, this chapter will also explain how to quickly, safely, and affordably rid your body of any harmful viruses, bacteria or parasites you have or may acquire.

Bag of Dirty Water

Picture your body as a bag of water. This shouldn't be much of a stretch, since our bodies are two thirds water. Now imagine that this bag of water has accumulated a great deal of silt or debris over the years. For many of us, the debris will have settled into our fatty tissue and is contributing to us being overweight. For many of us, the debris will have also settled into our joints and may be contributing to arthritis. For others the debris will have settled in another area and is contributing to another specific health concern.

Clearing Toxins

In order to get the toxins out of the areas where they have settled, we have to stir things up. Picture again our body as a bag of water with silt on the bottom. As we stir the water, the silt will begin to get mixed into the water—this is the result we want, as it will allow the body to clear the toxins. As with many things though, when it comes to detoxification, faster may not necessarily be better. We want to stir things up only as fast as our bodies can comfortably clear the toxins.

If we stir up settled toxins faster than our bodies can eliminate them, we experience an uncomfortable process known as a detox reaction or healing crisis. A healing crisis can often involve a temporary worsening of existing symptoms, headache, fatigue, or flu-like symptoms. While a healing crisis is a good sign that detoxification is occurring, it is not a pleasant experience and can be avoided.

Avoiding a Healing Crisis

It is preferable to avoid an uncomfortable healing crisis in the first place, and one of the best ways to do this is to keep our channels of elimination functioning optimally and support our immune systems while we detoxify. However, if detox symptoms are ever experienced, one of the fastest ways to eliminate the symptoms is to perform an Internal Body Wash to rinse out the colon.

To ensure we are clearing toxins from the body optimally, follow the guidelines set out in chapter 1 so that the frequency of bowel movements is increased to two or preferably three times daily. Since the colon is the primary channel of elimination and is so closely tied to the liver, regular bowel movements are very important.

Another way to ensure we are optimally clearing toxins is to drink plenty of water. Encouraging perspiration through exercise, steam, sauna, or a detox bath are other ways to increase the rate at which our bodies clear the toxins we are stirring up.

Supporting the Immune System

Supporting the immune system throughout the detoxification process is another way to ensure the process is a comfortable one.

Reducing the intake of sugar, alcohol, caffeine, and fried foods while increasing the intake of freshly squeezed juice and raw produce is helpful. Sugar intake is best avoided, primarily because it disables the immune system for several hours every time it is consumed. Alcohol is poisonous, acid-forming, and a depressant—all good reasons to reduce its intake. Caffeine is acid-forming and adds an unnecessary burden on the nervous system and adrenal glands. Deep-fried foods are a heavy strain on digestion and their fats are harmful to the body. Making healthy food and beverage decisions is definitely beneficial to support a healthy immune system.

There are also many excellent herbs and supplements that support the immune system—these include Moducare, Cold-FX, and herbal blends which include echinacea, goldenseal, and astragalus. Increasing your intake of vitamin C may also prove helpful throughout the detoxification process.

Taking several grams of vitamin C per day supplemented with Moducare is an excellent choice to begin with. Vitamin C is not only an excellent antioxidant, but also supports tissue repair and can even have a desirable laxative effect.

Moducare is an excellent choice because this product modulates the immune system, meaning it can adjust immune activity up or down. Most other immune related products only stimulate one's immune system, which can be detrimental if a person has an autoimmune disorder with an overactive immune system. Moducare was nothing short of a miracle for me when my health was hitting rock bottom. Two pleasant side-effects of taking Moducare are that it often boosts sexual stamina and reduces the symptoms of allergies.

Taking Out the Trash

Now that we've addressed how to make the detoxification process a comfortable one, we can take out the trash. Let's start by knocking out any unwanted viruses, bacteria, and parasites that might be undermining our health.

Viruses and Parasites

Viruses are a hot topic these days with the fear of a flu pandemic and the AIDS virus killing millions of people each year. Since we live in the age of antibiotics, many people are aware that the body often harbors infectious bacteria. What most people don't realize is how prevalent parasites are. Many people believe parasites are only a problem in impoverished countries or may associate parasites exclusively with large ones such as tape worms. The truth of the matter is that we all have parasites living within us and reducing their population is critical if you want to take control of your health.

Best-selling author of the book *The Cure For All Diseases* (New Century Press, 1993) Dr. Hulda Clark has identified and extensively documented the prevalence of parasites in today's society and how particular parasites relate to disease. For instance, in all cases of cancer, Clark has found a particular liver fluke present. According to Clark, by ridding the body of the relevant parasites, malignant cancers are immediately rendered benign.

As a service to humanity, Dr. Clark has generously allowed free copyright on all her books for non-commercial purposes. You can read her first book in its entirety online at CraigBrockie.com/Clark and you can also check out links to some of her other books which include books specific to cancer and HIV/AIDS treatments.

Candida

A parasite that we all play host to—whether we like it or not—is called Candida Albicans. Candida is a yeast organism (in other words, a fungus) and is kept in check by a healthy immune system with a healthy digestive tract. Unfortunately, healthy digestive tracts have become the exception rather than the rule. Standard American diets, combined with high levels of stress and antibiotic use, have left us vulnerable to Candida overgrowth. I've yet to meet a person who, when tested in a naturopathic clinic, didn't have Candida overgrowth, so if you think this doesn't apply to you, think again.

A healthy digestive tract will have at least 85% good bacteria. Unfortunately, as little as one round of antibiotic use can knock down the population of good bacteria and allow Candida to get the upper hand, and the more regularly you take antibiotics and the poorer your diet is, the more that Candida will flourish. If you're concerned about Candida overgrowth, then you will benefit from getting yourself tested by a naturopathic physician. Alternatively, you could simply assume that you have Candida overgrowth and start taking remedial action.

What's so bad about Candida? Well for starters, Candida coats the inside of our small intestine, preventing us from absorbing nutrients from the food we consume. This leaves us nutrient deficient and susceptible to disease. The overgrowth of Candida and the lack of nutrients also add to weight problems, by giving us cravings for more food.

Beyond the disruption to the biochemical balance, the Candida organisms excrete waste, increasing our levels of toxicity which can also inflame the small intestine and further undermine our health.

If left long enough, Candida roots itself deeply and can cause the small intestine to develop holes, leading to a condition called leaky gut syndrome. Leaky gut is what I suffered from in my early twenties and explained my lack of immunity, my fatigue, and my chronic sickness. Leaky gut has been found to be strongly correlated to the conditions fibromyalgia and Chronic Fatigue Symptom. If you or a loved one suffers either of these two conditions, then I suggest you consider a treatment for Candida and the treatments to heal the gut which are set out in the next chapter.

Bacteria

Bacteria get a bad rap. These organisms are generally associated with germs and sickness. However, like most things, bacteria are neither good nor bad in absolute terms.

Our bodies are covered with bacteria all the time and many of these bacteria have a beneficial effect. For instance, bacteria in the gut are essential to support proper digestive health and a strong immune system.

Antibiotics

Antibiotics kill bacteria, but they are non-selective—in other words, they kill all bacteria, whether good or bad. This is like spraying a non-selective weed killer on your lawn to kill a few dandelions—you kill the dandelions, but all the grass dies too.

After taking the antibiotic tetracycline for several months in high school to keep acne in check, I noticed my immune system had difficulty healing a simple scrape or cut. I was also sick more often than not, and living with chronic pain and unmanageable anxiety levels. For me, it was a simple process to reduce my Candida levels, which had risen due to my use of antibiotics. This reduction had such an incredible and immediate impact on my health that I clearly understand why reducing Candida overgrowth is often the first thing naturopathic doctors address.

Probiotics

Simply killing off the Candida in our digestive system is not enough to allow good bacteria to flourish. Good bacteria must be replenished.

You might have noticed yogurt in the supermarket which is listed as having active bacterial cultures. These bacterial cultures are the good bacteria we are talking about. A good probiotic supplement will be found in health stores in the refrigerator to keep the cultures alive. The probiotic supplement I've had the most success with is a product called Bio-K+, which is found in a liquid form in small 100 gram containers. Another range of probiotic supplements worth considering are called soil-based organisms.

Removing Candida

Ridding our bodies of excess Candida is easy, safe, and affordable.

While dietary changes are helpful, they are not necessary to get started. As you reduce your Candida levels you'll notice your cravings subside and it will be easier to adhere to a healthier diet. In the meantime, let's begin knocking out the Candida using supplementation.

My hands-down favorite supplement for killing Candida is oil of oregano in capsule form. Oil of oregano is found most commonly as a liquid, but is extremely spicy and has an unpleasant aftertaste, which is why I prefer capsules. Another reason I like oil of oregano so much is because it is a strong immune system stimulant, helping to support the body as it detoxifies.

I also consider oil of oregano to be the bazooka of flu remedies. If you're prone to or concerned about the flu and not in a position to invest in a medical ozone generator for your home, you'll want to keep oil of oregano capsules on hand. Oil of oregano effectively kills harmful viruses, bacteria, and other parasites, giving you many benefits all in one source.

It usually takes two to three months to reduce Candida to a healthy level. Like all organisms,

Candida is adaptive, therefore it is advisable to change supplements every couple of weeks when killing off Candida. After about 14 days of taking oil of oregano capsules, try taking another Candida elimination product such as grapefruit seed extract capsules, caprylic acid, or another product known for this purpose. You can return to oil of oregano after 14 days of taking another product if you choose to.

Killing off the Candida in your system is best taken at a comfortable pace. Candida creates toxicity inside our body while the organisms are alive and also creates toxicity as they die off. If you ever begin to experience symptoms of a healing crisis, reducing your daily dosage of Candida killer is advisable. Keeping your bowels moving two or three times daily throughout this process is important too. If you do happen to begin to experience symptoms of a detox reaction, remember that the Internal Body Wash is one of the fastest and most effective ways to overcome this condition.

Once you begin to reduce your Candida levels, you are likely to feel better in all areas of your life, including your mental and emotional health. Candida has such a systemic effect in undermining one's overall wellness that removing it from your body is something you'll truly be happy you did.

Calling for Trash Collection

It is fundamental to our well-being and basic common sense that harmful toxins be removed from our bodies. You wouldn't knowingly eat a sandwich full of parasites and toxins, so why would you tolerate their existence in your gut? And like so many of the treatments in this book, the action you need to take is quite straightforward, but the results can be dramatic.

In this chapter, we have focused on knocking out some of the worst health offenders. We have left the cleansing of specific organs—as well as cleansing the lymphatic system, kidneys, liver, and fatty tissue—to the next chapter.

Chapter 6
Healing from the Inside Out

If you have taken action on the suggestions found in previous chapters, chances are you're feeling much better than you did previously. Let's use this positive momentum to continue on the path to greater wellness.

By now your symptoms have likely lessened, your energy levels are probably higher, and your weight and appearance have likely improved. You are probably enjoying improvements in your mental and emotional health as well. Congratulations!

There's no time like the present to complete another health assessment to quantify your progress and identify the areas you still wish to experience improvement. Go to CraigBrockie.com/TakeControl where you can download copies of the Winners

Keep Score health assessment from. You can check on your progress by regularly completing this assessment. I encourage you to share copies of the assessment with your friends and family so they can keep track of their health.

Once we've begun rinsing ourselves out and taking out the trash, we're ready to begin healing ourselves from the inside out.

Understanding Enzymes

Previously our digestive tract was coated with compacted fecal matter, excess mucus, and Candida. Now that we've stripped out much of the junk, we may find our digestive tracts more sensitive than they once were. Not to worry, we will soon be coating our insides with immune-boosting good bacteria, soothing inflammation, and desensitizing ourselves to substances that may currently be allergens.

One of the easiest things we can do to bolster our digestion and begin healing from the inside is to understand the importance of enzymes. Enzymes are proteins that help us digest our food—without enzymes, we cannot properly extract all the necessary energy from what we eat. Without sufficient enzymes we are also putting additional strain on our bodies (in particular our pancreas) leading to residual health issues. This is compounded by the increased amount of food we are consuming to compensate for poor energy extraction, which means the pancreas has to do *even more* work.

But enzymes have much greater significance than may be implied by their primary role as a catalyst to help in the digestion of food. Specifically, enzymes are necessary for every chemical action that takes place in our body, including the immune system and the digestive system. Enzymes run all of our body's tissue, so they are vital in every cell of our muscles, bones, and organs. Our stamina and our energy levels are governed by enzymes. Even the rate at which we age is governed by enzymes, and most significantly our lifespan is governed by enzymes. When the body has exhausted its enzyme potential, future life expectancy is greatly reduced.

Many factors affect enzymes, for instance, cooking destroys enzymes. Temperatures above 116° Fahrenheit (47° Celsius) kill all enzymes.

So the answer is raw food, right?

Not necessarily. Even the raw vegetables and fruits we eat may be enzyme-deficient! Raw produce can be excellent natural sources of enzymes but unfortunately, they contain few enzymes when they are picked green, which is often the case because of long-distance transportation. Enzymes develop as plants ripen in soil. Irradiation also destroys enzymes.

But all is not lost; there are many things we can do to increase enzymes and enhance the effectiveness of enzymes. For instance, I take plant-based digestive enzyme capsules with almost every meal. Unpasteurized apple cider vinegar, fresh lemon juice, and fresh lime juice are also all rich in enzymes and can aid the digestion of our food, especially if taken before meals or included as part of the meal. Also, we can put greater emphasis on raw produce, seeds, and nuts. In order to ensure that our raw food has those beneficial enzymes, we can look to buy locally produced food, which is likely to have stayed in the soil for longer since it won't have been transported so far and is less likely to have been irradiated.

Digestive enzymes can eliminate the feeling of bloating and digestive discomfort. If taking digestive enzymes before meals doesn't eliminate the discomfort, then there are two other things to consider:

- Food sensitivities.
- Food combining.

Let's look at both of these in a bit more detail.

Food Sensitivities

Food sensitivities are more subtle than allergies.

While known allergies may cause a dramatic response such as skin rashes or sneezing, food sensitivities generally do not. For this reason, you've likely been consuming foods you are sensitive to for many years and not even known it. Rather than creating a dramatic response, food sensitivities undermine our health as a whole by aggravating our known symptoms of disease and putting unnecessary strain on our immune systems. Food sensitivities also cause us to retain excess water which makes us look puffy and less attractive.

Now that we've cleaned out most of the slimy, toxin-laden mucus that was coating our digestive tracts, when we consume foods we are sensitive to, the response may become more obvious. Common responses are bloating, gas, or a more obvious aggravation of our symptoms of disease.

In the short term, the best course of action is to temporarily avoid the foods we are sensitive to. The good news is that it's common for people to instantly lose five to ten pounds of puffy water weight, simply from doing so. Avoiding food sensitivities also helps us avoid digestive discomfort, gives our immune system a much-needed break, and stops aggravating our symptoms of disease. All these benefits give our bodies more resources to heal.

The other good news is that food sensitivities will lessen or even disappear entirely just from giving our bodies a break from the constant burden. You could think of food sensitivities as a mildly annoying person. If we allow an irritating person to hang with us day-in and day-out, they are bound to cause us grief. However, if we give ourselves a break, as little as a few weeks away might be enough for us to begin to find humor in their behavior and develop strategies for dealing with the person so they no longer bother us.

Later in the chapter I'll share with you two secrets we can use to desensitize ourselves to food sensitivities and in many cases permanently eliminate full-blown allergies. In the meantime, let's discuss how to easily and effectively determine what foods we are sensitive to.

While strong allergies can be determined by medical doctors using a common scratch test, food sensitivities are generally too subtle to be detected this way. Fortunately, the advanced field of energy medicine offers quick, safe, and affordable assessment methods

- A holistic allergist or naturopathic doctor practicing electrodermal testing can quickly scan the body for dozens of common food and environmental sensitivities.

- If you do not have access to electrodermal testing, applied kinesiology can be used to go through your fridge and pantry to quickly determine which foods to avoid. We first introduced applied kinesiology in chapter 2—it uses simple muscle biofeedback to determine what things weaken us and which do not.

- A less subjective method to determine food sensitivities involves sending a blood sample off to a lab for blood antibody allergy testing.

Some common allergens you'll want to make sure you test are dust, dust mites, mold, pets, dairy products, wheat, and sugar. Also be sure to test anything you consume regularly, as the body often has difficulty processing things it's not given a break from. For instance, while sensitivity to rice is uncommon in North America, sensitivity to rice far more common in Asia due to its regular consumption there.

If emphasizing raw foods in your diet, taking digestive enzymes with meals, and avoiding food sensitivities is not enough to address all your digestive concerns, then we need to look at food combining.

Food Combining

Food combining is a concept that was introduced to me by Dr. Darrell Wolfe.

Dr. Wolfe is an expert in regaining health through healing from the inside out. Not only does he provide a great deal of excellent educational information on his website (thewolfeclinic.com), his clinic provides one-on-one telephone health consultations to patients all over the world.

Dr. Wolfe does a great job on his website of explaining which foods are best combined in the same meal and which combinations should be avoided to ensure optimal digestion and comfort. For instance, eating a meal with both protein and starches makes for a challenging digestive burden. Follow this meal up with a sugary dessert, and gas, bloating, and discomfort are a likely outcome.

Taking probiotics and enzymes, avoiding food sensitivities, and following food combining guidelines will help reduce inflammation in the gut and therefore provide the digestive tract an opportunity to heal.

What Should I Eat?

So what should we all be eating?

The short answer to this question is that no one (that I'm aware of) knows for sure what the ideal diet for humans is. While there are strong arguments for vegetarianism, raw food, diets based on one's blood type, "The Zone" and other fashionable diets, there are many conflicting opinions. However, there are some commonsense approaches where there seems to be something of a consensus:

- Drink two or more liters of filtered, preferably alkaline water throughout each day.
- Reduce intake of caffeine, alcohol, sugar, simple carbohydrates, highly processed, and fried foods.

- Emphasize intake of alkalizing foods, fresh produce, and omega rich oils.

- Take time and relax at meal time, and chew food thoroughly.

- Minimize beverage intake—even water—during meals to avoid diluting digestive enzymes.

Emphasizing certified organic products is also a very wise choice. I highly recommend watching the movie *Food Inc.* if you question this logic. I also suggest you do your homework about microwave ovens. A great deal of evidence suggests that microwaved foods can be very detrimental to our health.

What Supplements Should I Take?

Once we've taken out the trash and the gut is in repair, our nutrient absorption will be much higher than it was previously. It is therefore now a good time to discuss supplementation.

If your gut has been damaged (and that is likely with the amount of trash that most of us have had to get rid of), you can speed recovery by supplementing with l-glutamine and aloe vera juice, which will help to soothe and repair the gut. Continuing to use digestive enzymes and probiotics is also important while the body recovers.

Looking at nutrients, some quick research on soil mineral depletion, the source of conventional fertilizers (hint: it's petroleum), and the prolific use of poisonous chemicals on our crops can lead one to believe that our food supply could in fact be deficient in some critical nutrients and perhaps could be providing more harm to us than good. A series of tests at a naturopathic clinic can uncover our specific nutritional deficiencies. However, even without knowing the specifics, there are some supplements that most people can benefit from replenishing.

Minerals

If you are too acidic, have pain, anxiety, depression, or constipation, you are likely to be magnesium deficient. If your body has depleted its magnesium stores, it's also likely that calcium levels have also been depleted. Both symptoms are a result of acidosis (see chapter 4). Potassium, zinc, and many other minerals that are found in nature in trace amounts are also important.

As mentioned in earlier chapters, ionic minerals are the most absorbable form to use for supplementation.

Vitamins

Consuming freshly prepared (not-pasteurized) juice is a great way to get enzymes and a broad spectrum of vitamins. Next to juicing, whole food supplements such as powdered green products are an excellent way to get a full spectrum of vitamins in natural form. Most multi-vitamin products consist of artificial vitamins and are therefore a less desirable alternative.

When it comes to RDAs (recommended daily allowances), forget about these!! Take supplements as directed on the bottle and gradually increase dosages to double or triple the recommended dosages for a 3 to 6 week period to overcome years of accumulated nutrient deficiencies and gain the full benefit.

If you drink alcohol or often feel stressed out, you are likely deficient in B vitamins. B vitamins are water-soluble, which means they need to be taken daily since they don't hang around in your system the way fat-soluble vitamins do.

Dr. Joseph Mercola (mercola.com) presents a great deal of research that suggests most people are deficient in vitamin D and benefit from maximizing exposure to sunlight in addition to further supplementation.

Antioxidants

Antioxidants are a common buzzword these days. If you research antioxidants online or get invited to an MLM (network marketing) meeting you'll find many products claiming to be the best antioxidant available to mankind. When you encounter these claims, run away as the products are usually overpriced, the health claims overstated, and the "business opportunities" questionable.

Oxidation Reduction Potential (ORP) is the only objective way to measure a product's ability to reduce oxidation that I'm aware of. And when it comes to ORP, alkaline water from a good quality water ionizer provides ORP readings in a league of their own when compared with any other natural antioxidant source. That said, continuing to supplement with vitamin C is a wise choice. Further antioxidants will be gained from juicing and whole food supplements. Consuming additional antioxidants, while not detrimental, may only be necessary for those unable to afford a water ionizer.

24-Hour Liver Flush

I now want to tell you how you can eliminate allergies and chronic pain with a 24-Hour Liver Flush. This procedure is based on the book *The Cure for All Diseases* (New Century Press, 1993) by Dr. Hulda Clark. Check out CraigBrockie.com/Clark where you can find online support for this procedure.

Before we continue, you may be wondering whether the liver cleanse is safe. According to Dr. Clark it is very safe and this assertion is based on over 500 cases, including many people in their seventies and eighties. None went to the hospital and none even reported pain. Most people feel great immediately afterwards, but a few can feel ill for one or two days later. If you feel ill, consider completing a parasite cleansing program before completing your next liver cleanse.

While the program is safe, you should never consider a liver flush when you are acutely ill.

Cleansing the liver of gallstones dramatically improves digestion, which is the basis of your whole health. You can expect your allergies to disappear, too—more with each cleanse you do! Incredibly, it also eliminates shoulder, upper arm, and upper back pain and you will have more energy coupled with an increased sense of wellness.

It is the job of the liver to make bile: 1 to 1½ liters in a day! The liver is full of tubes (biliary tubing) that deliver the bile to one large tube (the common bile duct). The gallbladder is attached to the common bile duct and acts as a storage reservoir. Eating fat or protein triggers the gallbladder to squeeze itself empty after about twenty minutes and the stored bile finishes its trip down the common bile duct to the intestine.

For many people, including children, the biliary tubing is choked with gallstones. Some develop allergies or hives but some have no symptoms. When the gallbladder is scanned or X-rayed nothing is seen because the stones are not in the gallbladder. Not only that, most are too small and are not calcified, a prerequisite for visibility on X-ray.

There are over half a dozen varieties of gallstones,

most of which have cholesterol crystals in them. They can be black, red, white, green, or tan colored. The green ones get their color from being coated with bile. At the very center of each stone is found a clump of bacteria, suggesting that a dead bit of parasite might have started the stone forming.

As the stones grow and become more numerous, the pressure on the liver causes it to make less bile. It is also thought to slow the flow of lymphatic fluid. Imagine the situation if your garden hose had marbles in it. Much less water would flow, which in turn would decrease the ability of the hose to squirt out the marbles. With gallstones, much less cholesterol leaves the body, and cholesterol levels may rise.

Added to which, gallstones are porous and so can pick up all the bacteria, cyst viruses, and parasites that are passing through the liver. In this way, "nests" of infection are formed, forever supplying the body with fresh bacteria and parasites. Stomach infection—such as ulcers or intestinal bloating—cannot be cured permanently without removing these gallstones from the liver.

One way to remove these gallstones is by following this 24-Hour Liver Flush.

Ingredients

You will need the following ingredients:

- Epsom salts—4 tablespoons.

- Apple juice (or water for diabetics)—3 cups. Apple juice hides the taste of the Epsom salts and contains malic acid, which is known to help soften gallstones.

- Your favorite nut, seed, or olive oil—½ cup.

- 1 or 2 pink grapefruit or 3 to 6 lemons (enough to squeeze between 2/3 and 3/4 of a cup of juice).

- A herbal sleep aid (available at most health food stores). You need to have enough to ensure you sleep: don't skip this or you may have an uncomfortable night.

- A large plastic straw (to help you drink your remedy).

- A pint jar with a lid.

Directions

Choose a day for the liver flush when you will be able to rest on the following day.

Take no medicines, vitamins, or pills that you can do without, as they could prevent success. Eat a no-fat, low protein breakfast and lunch, such as cooked cereal, fruit, fruit juice, bread, and preserves or honey (no butter or milk). This allows the bile to build up and develop pressure in the liver. Higher pressure pushes out more stones.

Start the process 8 hours before you go to bed. For this example, I'm assuming a 10pm bed time.

2:00pm. Do not eat or drink after 2 o'clock in the afternoon. Do not even drink water, so you will want to ensure you are well hydrated before this time. If you do not follow this rule you could feel quite ill later.

Take your Epsom salts and mix with your apple juice (or water) and pour this into a container. This makes four servings of ¾ cup. Set the container in the refrigerator to get ice cold (this is for convenience and taste only).

6:00pm. Drink one serving of ¾ cup (one-quarter of the ice cold Epsom salts mixture).

8:00pm. Repeat by drinking another ¾ cup (one-quarter of the Epsom salts mixture). You won't have eaten since two o'clock, but you shouldn't feel hungry.

At this time it is best get your bedtime chores done—the timing of the process is critical for success.

9:45pm. Pour the oil (½ cup, measured) into the pint jar. Wash your grapefruit (or lemons) in hot water and dry, then squeeze into a measuring cup and remove the pulp with fork. You should have at least ½ cup but ¾ cup is better. You may add the juice of one orange for a better taste. Add the grapefruit (or lemons and orange) to the oil. Close the jar tightly with the lid and shake hard until the mixture is watery.

Now visit the bathroom one or more times, even if it makes you late for your ten o'clock drink, but don't be more than 15 minutes late, as you will get fewer stones.

10:00pm. Drink the oil and citrus potion you have just mixed. Take your herbal sleep aid with the first sips to make sure you will sleep through the night.

Drinking through a large plastic straw often helps the mixture go down more easily. You may also use honey, brown sugar, or candied ginger to chase down the mixture. Take it to your bedside if you want, but drink it standing up and get it down within 5 minutes (fifteen minutes for very elderly or weak individuals).

Once you have finished the mixture, lie down immediately. You might not see complete success (in other words, you may fail to get stones out) if you don't. The sooner you lie down the more stones you will get out.

Be ready for bed ahead of time. Don't clean up the kitchen... don't waste time doing anything else—as soon as the drink is down, walk to your bed and lie down flat on your back with your head up high on the pillow. Try to think about what is happening in your liver. Try to keep perfectly still for at least

20 minutes. You may feel a train of stones traveling along the bile ducts like marbles. There is no pain because the bile duct valves are open thanks to the Epsom salts.

The next step should be easy: go to sleep.

Next morning. Upon waking, take your third dose of Epsom salts mixture, but don't take this dose before 6:00am. If you have indigestion or nausea, wait until this has passed before drinking the Epsom salts. You may go back to bed or get on with your day, but be sure to stay close to a bathroom at all times. If you are feeling dehydrated, sip a glass of water or two.

2 hours later. Take your fourth (the last) dose of Epsom salts mixture. You may go back to bed again if you so choose.

30 minutes later (optional). If you'd like to thoroughly rinse your entire digestive tract, including the colon, now is an ideal time to begin drinking more water.

The water you drink over the next hour will flush right through your body, exiting very quickly. This creates a similar effect and benefit to the Internal Body Wash explained in chapter 1. Every 10 to 15 minutes you can drink another large glass or two of water and thoroughly rinse your body from the inside out. Within an hour, you'll be eliminating water that is perfectly clear!

After 2 more hours you may eat. Start with fruit juice. Half an hour later eat fruit. One hour later you may eat regular food but keep it light. By supper you should feel recovered.

How Well Did You Do?

Expect diarrhea in the morning.

Use a flashlight to look for gallstones in the toilet with the bowel movement. Look for the green kind since this is proof that they are genuine gallstones, not food residue. Only bile from the liver is pea green. The bowel movement sinks but gallstones float because of the cholesterol inside.

Count them all roughly, whether tan or green. You will need to total 2,000 stones before the liver is clean enough to rid you of allergies or bursitis or upper back pains permanently. The first cleanse may rid you of them for a few days, but as the stones from the rear travel forward, they will give you the same symptoms again and so you are likely need to repeat this cleanse several times, with a minimum interval between treatments of two weeks.

Sometimes the bile ducts are full of cholesterol crystals that did not form into round stones. These appear as "chaff" floating on top of the toilet bowl water. They may be tan colored and harboring millions of tiny white crystals. Cleansing this chaff is just as important as purging the stones.

Congratulations

You have taken out your gallstones without surgery! While this liver flush protocol was popularized by Dr. Hulda Clark, it was invented hundreds, if not thousands, of years ago by herbalists.

Take Action!

Of all the topics I talk about, the 24-Hour Liver Flush is often the one that gains the most interest.

Most people understand the importance of their liver in detoxifying their bodies. Those who like to indulge in alcohol from time to time especially appreciate the idea of cleaning out their liver. Although the 24-Hour Liver Flush gains so much interest, I've found that very few people follow through and actually try the protocol. For this reason, I've made a commitment to volunteer the third Saturday of every month to complete a 24-Hour Liver Flush with anyone who wishes to participate. You can also go to Forums.CraigBrockie.com for support and talk to others following a liver flush at the same time.

Permanent and Fast Allergy Elimination

Although completing several 24-Hour Liver Flushes is something you'll be glad you did, you may wish to fast-track the elimination of your food sensitivities and allergies. The benefit of this action is that you will remove the underlying burden on your immune system and reduce the aggravation of your symptoms without having to change your environment or eating habits.

For instance, it's one thing to know you're sensitive to wheat or dairy, but consistently avoiding these foods is challenging. And if you happen to be allergic to dust, dust mites, or your own pet, avoiding these allergens may not be a reasonable expectation. Thankfully, solutions exist.

If you have a few hundred dollars to invest in your health, I highly recommend getting treated by a holistic allergist. There are two advanced holistic allergy elimination protocols. The more well known of the two is called NAET (Nambudripad's Allergy Elimination Technique). A newer and more direct approach is called Bioenergetic Intolerance Elimination or BIE. I chose BIE over NAET because BIE requires fewer visits to eliminate all of one's allergies—often four visits or fewer to get rid of them all, permanently.

BIE has been an absolute miracle for our family. Prior to BIE, our children were sensitive to wheat, dairy, soy, and even our dog. Keeping them healthy was a challenge for all of us. After just one BIE treatment, we noticed a dramatic improvement in their health. It was also great not to have to watch their diets so carefully. Treat foods like pizza and ice cream, which would often trigger symptoms previously, are no longer a concern.

If you have the resources available, I highly recommend you get treated by a holistic allergist as soon as possible since allergies and sensitivities are so detrimental to the healing process. There's no need to complete anything else first.

At CraigBrockie.com/Healing you'll find links for more information about holistic allergy treatments.

Cleansing the Lymph

The lymph system is the body's sewer—and there is more fluid in your lymph system than you have blood in your body (in other words, this is a significant part of your body that we're talking about). However, lymph systems are coming under increased pressure and the incidences of lymphatic cancer are rising.

One of the best treatments to support your lymph system is exercise. The most beneficial exercises are jogging, skipping (with a rope), and rebounding (bouncing, jogging, or dancing on a mini-trampoline).

Another approach you might consider is taking a homeopathic lymph diarrheal which is a diuretic for the lymphatic system.

Rebuilding the Adrenal Glands

If you've been under a lot of stress, your adrenal glands are likely exhausted.

As a first step you will probably find it helpful to reduce the intake of coffee and other stimulants. You might also want to revisit chapter 2 to check out strategies that work for you to reduce your stress levels. You might also look into adrenal extracts to speed the recovery of the adrenal glands.

Cleansing the Fat

There are toxins and there are toxins…

Some toxins are fat soluble—in other words, they are stored in the body's fat reserves—while others are water soluble, meaning that they are more likely to be present in the other fluid within our bodies.

Niacin, or vitamin B3 as it is more commonly called, is a vitamin which is an absolute miracle supplement for anyone with a heart or circulation condition. Niacin not only reduces cholesterol but when taken in higher doses creates a desirable "flushing" effect, which temporarily super-charges one's circulation. Niacin is also one of the best ways to start clearing out the fat. Another very simple approach is a sauna, which can help you sweat out the toxins.

Hubbard Sauna Protocol

Many of our problems are emotion-related and once a patient gets onto medication, all they do is look for the right combination of medications rather than try to address the underlying source of the problem. However, once the source has been identified and remedied, it's important to remove chemical residues from the body.

A profound treatment I think everyone would benefit knowing about is called the Hubbard Sauna Protocol (also known as the Purification Program). This protocol is extremely effective for helping individuals get drug and chemical residues out of their body using high doses of niacin, jogging, sauna, and supplementation.

In many ways, this is perhaps the ultimate detoxification program. In addition to clearing toxins from the fat and lymph, in my opinion, there's no better way to improve the health of one's skin. It's like showering the entire surface of your body from the inside out, with all the sweating involved.

The treatment is set out in the book *Clear Body Clear Mind* by L. Ron Hubbard (Bridge Publications, 2002). I completed my sauna program at home with a couple of close friends, using our infrared sauna. We all experienced dramatic improvements in our physical, mental, and emotional health from undertaking the program.

Dental Clean-Up

It is well accepted that heavy metals have a detrimental effect on our health.

One of the main ways that we introduce heavy metals into our systems is through the mercury in amalgam fillings in our teeth. The movie *The Beautiful Truth* (thebeautifultruthmovie.com) scientifically demonstrates how the discharge of gas from mercury-based fillings continues for many years after the filling has been put into a cavity.

In addition to the mercury that's in our teeth, there can be infection under the teeth. When an infection is trapped under a tooth, the immune system is always fighting the infection, leaving fewer resources available to heal the rest of the body.

To get our health under control it is important to address both issues in our mouth. A qualified biological dentist offers the best solution for *safely* replacing amalgam fillings and addressing chronic dental infections.

Chelation

Intravenous chelation therapy is an approach intended to strip out heavy metals from your system. Chelation therapy is affordable when compared to most conventional medical treatments, but since it is not something covered by health insurance, many people may be unable to afford chelation treatments.

Fortunately, several oral chelation options exist, including cilantro, apple cider vinegar, chlorella, and other safe and natural substances.

Feeling Clean on the Inside

Clearly, some of the suggestions in this chapter are more dramatic than the other treatments that we have looked at earlier in this book—in particular, the liver flush. We have covered a lot of different treatments which are all significant processes to move our health forward. Again you are reminded to take things at your own pace, research and implement what resonates with you when you are ready. For the next chapter, we are going to shift our focus from looking at internal cleaning to looking at pain, and more particularly, the causes of pain.

Chapter 7
Pain Elimination

When it comes to pain, I can relate. I lived with chronic pain for most of my twenties and know just how unpleasant it is. Fortunately chronic pain is now a distant memory for me and it can be for you too. Whether you suffer from arthritis, back pain, or a "bum" knee, you'll find helpful solutions in this chapter.

There are three main causes of pain:

- biochemical
- structural, and
- energetic.

We'll discuss all three causes and how to quickly, safely, and affordably rid ourselves once and for all of chronic pain.

Biochemical Causes of Pain

We've already discussed biochemical health—the main concepts we looked at were:

- pH
- toxicity, and
- nutrition.

Let's briefly revisit these concepts, starting with pH.

If our blood becomes too acidic, we could die. Thankfully, our bodies are too smart to just give up and die, so when we become too acidic our body begins to rob our muscles and bones of minerals such as magnesium and calcium. We perceive this removal of calcium and magnesium as pain.

Both minerals are alkaline, which helps neutralize the acidity, but they also have other important functions within the body:

- Calcium creates a tightening effect inside the body which helps make bones denser, for instance. We've all heard the hype over the past few years about the importance of women taking calcium to help reduce the risks of osteoporosis. It's not surprising then that naturopathic medicine has found strong links between osteoporosis and acidosis, a condition where the body is chronically acidic and robbing the bones of calcium.

- As I've mentioned before in the book, magnesium has a loosening effect on the body. It helps muscles relax, which explains the relaxing effect of taking a hot bath with magnesium sulfate, otherwise known as Epsom salts. Painful muscles are invariably tight and represent areas of the body that are likely to be magnesium deficient.

Having acidosis is like the inside of your body being on fire. Consuming calcium and magnesium supplements is like trying to put out a fire with a squirt gun and doesn't address why your body is on fire in the first place, but if you are suffering from pain, in the short term, I highly recommend supplements with high doses of both minerals. To address the cause of your acidosis though, we need to address what is causing you to be acidic in the first place, and if you check back to chapter 4 you can follow the steps to becoming more alkaline.

As you would expect, toxicity is also a major cause of pain within the body. Take arthritis as one example—in essence, this disease is a result of toxic deposits settling in our joints and causing inflammation. So rather than treat the inflammation, it is far more practical to address the toxins that caused the problem in the first place by removing them from the body. Often the act of removing toxins from the body will reduce or eliminate the symptoms of arthritis.

Toxins are also typically acidic, and so while they remain within your body they contribute to a vicious cycle of pain and illness.

As I've mentioned in earlier chapters, when our bodies are under a lot of stress, they are usually nutrient deficient, and this deficiency goes beyond the basic minerals and vitamins. Again, this is another cause of pain, which can be addressed by supplementation.

We looked at enzymes in the last chapter. In addition to nutrients, enzymes are incredibly important in dealing with pain—when there are more enzymes in the body, all of the processes work better: inflammation is reduced, toxins are cleared more swiftly, and tissue can recover at a faster rate.

My Sulfur Miracle (MSM)

MSM (Methylsulfonylmethane) is another miracle supplement I'd like to introduce to you.

Those who suffer pain are usually sulfur deficient. MSM is not only a great antioxidant, but when taken in therapeutic dosages, it greatly reduces inflammation, speeds tissue repair, and creates an environment that allows higher oxygen saturation within the cells.

My experience with taking a therapeutic dose of MSM felt like my muscles were getting a bath from the inside out, washing away years of accumulated junk. Even scar tissue begins to noticeably soften within a day or two of beginning a therapeutic dose. Other positive benefits of MSM supplementation my family and I have experienced are improved respiratory health and increased athletic endurance.

Ed McCabe suggests a therapeutic dose of 500mg per 30lbs of body weight, taken twice daily. In other words, a 150lb person would take 2,500mg twice daily. This is the dosage I have used with outstanding results.

MSM is a close relative to DMSO (dimethyl sulfoxide) that I mentioned in chapter 3 as an excellent topical remedy, especially for those with herpes. DMSO is also great for relieving sore joints and muscles.

Acute Pain? Traumeel to the Rescue!

Traumeel is an amazing homeopathic product I'd like to see in every first aid kit.

Dr. Swetlikoff (who has kindly written the foreword to this book) first introduced me to Traumeel after I fell off my son's skateboard. I landed badly with all 220 lbs of my weight being concentrated on my elbow and my hip. My body was in shock; it was the most serious injury I'd had in years.

I was instructed to take one Traumeel tablet every 10 to 15 minutes for the first two hours and then one tablet every 3 to 5 hours until I was healed. He also gave me Traumeel cream to apply topically. Immediately after taking Traumeel the shock subsided.

The next day I awoke expecting to be bedridden with pain—I had never ever heard of Traumeel before and had not even applied ice to my injury. Instead I was in slight discomfort and ended up going on a lengthy bike ride.

While I would normally expect severe and long-lasting bruises, I barely bruised and recovered completely in about half the time with less than half the pain. Dr. Swetlikoff explained how these results are routine, and from my ongoing research and experience I agree.

Athletes, parents, and all first aid kits need to have Traumeel. I'm not compensated by Heel (the manufacturer of Traumeel) and provide this endorsement completely voluntarily.

Structural Pain: Feet

Moving on to structure-related pain, I like to take both a bottom-up and top-down view of the structure. Since a foundation is commonly considered most important to the stability of a building, and since it is less expensive to work from the ground up, let's start there first.

When you look down at your feet, consider how much they do for you: they take you everywhere that you go. Even more than your car, they are your transportation.

If your car tires are not fully inflated, there is more friction as you drive on the road, although it is hard to realize, as the engine is doing all of the work. However, when you are riding a bicycle it is a lot more apparent if there's more friction when the tires aren't fully inflated: more work is required. The same holds true for the feet.

Alignment of the Feet

One issue worth considering is the alignment of your feet and ankles. This issue is similar to the alignment of your tires.

If you are driving down the road and your car is veering off to one side, you would experience that problem through your steering wheel. However, you wouldn't blame the problem on the steering wheel—instead you would understand that something connected to the steering wheel, for instance your wheel alignment, would be the cause of the problem. The steering wheel would be the symptom but the misaligned wheels on the road would be the root cause.

With the body, we have a similar kind of situation. You might be feeling your pain in one part, but that pain may arise from somewhere else.

For instance, you might be feeling pain in your knees, lower back, or your neck, but these pains may be related to the alignment of your feet. If you go to a podiatrist, he or she can analyze your feet. Often, podiatrists take a mold of your feet and point out indicators of how flat or weak your feet are. But let's take a step back—we are dealing with feet, after all—stand up and take a look at your feet. Are they close to parallel or do your feet angle out (is there more than 10 or 20 degrees between your feet)? Remember what your feet look like as we continue with the chapter.

Flat Feet

Some of the most common foot-related conditions include weak or reduced arches and flat-footedness, both of which lead to pronation in your ankle.

When your arch is less than ideal, your foot collapses inwards towards the inside of your body, which puts stress on your ankle, and your toes angle towards the outside of your body to create a V-shape. Your feet should ideally be nearly parallel (but not perfectly parallel) and your ankles should be aligned directly above your heels (so that the center of your shin is over the center of your foot).

You might, however, see that your feet angle out and that your ankles seem to roll inwards. When this is the case, your condition is called pronation, the most common scenario for foot dysfunction. Pronation is far more common than supination, another dysfunction, which occurs when your arches are too high.

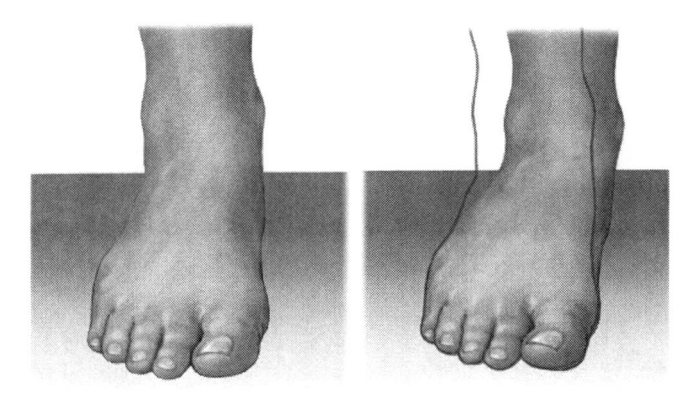

With the normal foot position (on the left) the weight is distributed evenly. When the foot position leads to excessive pronation (the image on the right), the weight of the body is placed over the inside edge of the foot.

Medical image copyright © 2009 Nucleus Medical Art (nucleusinc.com). All rights reserved.

Having your ankles rolled in due to pronation puts a great deal of stress on your knees. Your feet are like the wheels and your knees are like the axle of your body: the pivot point for your walking and running. When there is stress on your knees, that continues upwards into your system and adds stress to your hips. Your hips are like your suspension—the shock absorbers for your body. So when your

..., it is often due to stress in your feet, ...d knees leading to your hips becoming ...ed.

...never there is misalignment, the body typically tightens things up to try to provide support, but that creates more tightness in the muscles, and tight muscles are often painful. That's why it feels so much better when a massage therapist gets to work on your muscles and loosens them up.

Having tightness in your hips is like having shock absorbers that are stiff or seized. And when your feet are flat and out of alignment, that is like having underinflated and unaligned tires, which create a symptom that you'd feel in the steering wheel.

So let's think about how that same dysfunction occurs in your body. If your feet are flat and out of alignment, that puts stress on your feet, your ankles, and your knees, which in turn causes pain in your knees and often tightness in your hips. When your hips are tight, any kind of jarring movement (such as walking, running, or jumping) transmits directly upwards through your body into your back and can even affect your neck, shoulders, and arms.

Improving Our Feet

Fortunately there is an affordable, easy, and fast way to improve our feet.

There are two ways to deal with feet-related issues:

the first is to visit a podiatrist, who will usually analyze your stance, your foot, and how you step. The podiatrist may then custom make what are called orthotics (these are essentially braces that go inside your shoe to hold your foot in the correct angle and create an arch for you). Your health insurance may cover custom orthotics; check with your provider.

I have gone this route and I can assure you that you will experience a benefit from this. However, in my opinion, this approach does not address the root problem; it merely introduces a brace, and what I have found is that the arch that is formed this way is not permanent—you remove the orthodic and your foot goes flat again. It is better to strengthen the feet and regain the natural arch. In my case, I initially had flat feet that were size 15 (and, as you would imagine, a wide size 15 shoe is very difficult to find). My arch was almost completely gone, which actually explains the length of my foot—it was mashed out because it wasn't properly aligned.

I tried custom orthotics first, spending around $300 per pair. Unfortunately, it is a rather inconvenient technology; you can't use orthodics with sandals or flip-flops, and when you walk barefoot, there is no support. You will likely feel some benefit from orthotics, but my experience and research has led me to believe that orthotics do not treat the cause.

A less expensive and, in my experience, better solution (because it trains your foot to work without an orthodic) is to use a product called Barefoot Science. If you go to BarefootScience.com, you'll see a great introductory video that explains this technology. It is a foot-strengthening system that you insert into your shoes, and for only about $100, you can get three sets of these inserts. So instead of custom orthotics that you would have to transfer from one shoe to another, you can have three of your favorite pairs of shoes set up with this technology. And all you really have to do is wear the shoes.

The Barefoot Science system offers six stages of foot strengthening and works by stimulating the ball of your foot with an under-sole insert. Through this method, you gradually train your feet to regain their natural arch.

You start with a small insert that is very soft. After a couple of weeks, you will no longer feel that first insert, and that is when you move up and begin to use the second-level insert, which is a little higher and firmer.

You go through stages, wearing each insert for two to three weeks or as long as it takes before you no longer feel it, and then you move on to the next level of insert. Eventually you get to level six, which is a thick and firm insert. Once you get past level six and no longer feel the insert in your shoe, you will be able to stand normally, look down at your bare feet and find that:

- your natural arch has been regained and is stronger
- your feet are more parallel
- the alignment of your ankles has improved tremendously, and
- your toes are probably no longer angled out nearly as much as they were.

Personally, I went from a size 15 shoe size down to a 13—that's how much arch I regained by using this system. For a cost of around $100 in probably 8 to 12 weeks, you can regain your natural arch and take a tremendous amount of strain off your feet, your ankles, and your knees, which in turn will take a lot of stress off your hips and lower back.

Treating flattened feet is like inflating flat tires and getting a wheel alignment. If you address the root cause directly, you no longer feel symptoms further up the system in the steering wheel, or in terms of your body, in your knees, hips, neck, and shoulders.

If your health care plan includes podiatry, then you can see a podiatrist to be assessed. A less expensive option to confirm if you have pronation is to visit a store that specializes in running. Here in Canada there is a company called *The Running Room* that evaluates your gait and arch for free—check out the specialist stores close to you or in your nearest city.

In addition to reducing pain throughout the entire body, strengthening the feet greatly improves athlete performance. Pronation is a serious handicap for most sports, especially sports that involve foot speed, skating, or balance.

Structural Pain: Hips

So now let's move upwards through the body structure and look at our hips.

We have already made improvement to our hips by correcting our feet. This will have lessened the strain on our hips, but if you've been walking around with flat, unaligned tires for many years, there will likely be alignment issues with your hips as well and the muscles in there could be chronically tight.

A good place to start when you want to improve your hips is to get a really good deep tissue massage in your hip area from just below the rib cage down to the top of your thighs, front and back.

Another simple step to help release a lot of that tension is to lie on top of a basketball and roll it in and around the inside of your rib cage, and also press it right into your upper thighs. This is similar to the technique that we used in chapter 3, but involves applying the basketball to a wider area of the body.

Performing core strengthening exercises is also recommended. Remember, our hips are like our suspension, so if we are walking, jogging, or doing any kind of sport, we want our hips to be loose and strong so that they can respond healthily to whatever it is we are doing with our body. We want them to absorb a lot of the shock that our feet, ankles, and knees are experiencing. Otherwise, that shock will go right up our body and affect our lower back, mid-back, neck, and even our shoulders. And if there is a dysfunction in our shoulder, that can easily contribute to a dysfunction in our arms—the whole body is truly connected.

According to the Chinese, our body's energy center is located right below our navel, so strengthening this area of the body is also beneficial for our energy. There are many benefits to doing strengthening exercises for our abdominal area and hips, and keeping these muscles loose. One other (physical) exercise you can try is to lie face down on a mat, push your upper body up, and then look up and behind you. This helps you stretch the front of your body. A back bridge is another great exercise.

A lot of people feel pain in their backs, but nine times out of ten, it is not the muscles in their back that are causing that pain. Try watching people's feet as they walk by—I guarantee you will see a lot of people's feet angled out creating a V-shape and with ankles that are improperly aligned (suggesting fallen arches). This is more the norm than the exception, so once you get an eye for this, you will start noticing this condition more and more often, and now you will understand one of the reasons why many people feel pain in their everyday lives.

Structural Pain: Structural Alignment

When it comes to structural alignment above the waist, there are three common scenarios:

- kyphosis
- lordosis, and
- scoliosis.

These all have to do with spinal alignment.

Kyphosis

Kyphosis is the least common condition and is informally referred to as hunchback. While it is the least common, it is the easiest to notice—essentially, the top of the body and the head lean too far forward.

Lordosis

Lordosis (swayback) is far more common than kyphosis. With this condition, the lower back is too far back, or posterior as a doctor would describe it.

Scoliosis

Lastly, there is scoliosis, which is a twisting of the

spine. This is generally caused by the head being off to one side or the other.

Kyphosis and lordosis are normally a front/back issue, where scoliosis typically relates to your head being off to one side.

The Root Cause of Back Issues

We've already talked about our feet and our hips, so let's go right to the top: our head. The head weighs around 8 to 10 lbs (3½ to 4½ kg) and what typically happens if your head is out of alignment is that your body structure compensates; in particular the hips will move to compensate.

If you look into a mirror, you can probably see that your head is a little bit tilted to one side or that your posture is not ideal. Think about the amount of strain that is being put on your body. In fact, here's a good way to illustrate the issue: take a 10 lb (5 kg) dumbbell, extend it over your head, and keep the weight centered above your shoulder.

Notice that, once the weight is centered, it does not put a lot of strain on the body. Now hold the weight off to one side and you will feel it is out of alignment because more strain will be felt by the muscles throughout your body, and your shoulder will become strained by holding that non-aligned weight. Put the weight back to the center, and a lot of strain will be taken off of your system. The same holds true with your head—if it is just slightly out of alignment, it begins to put a strain on the whole system below and can lead to a lot of issues right down to your hips and feet.

With kyphosis (hunch back), the head is a little bit too far forward, which leads to the hips moving forward as well. The two actions cause the spine to bend, giving the characteristic appearance. If you can find a kyphosis sufferer and move their head back a little bit into proper alignment on top of the spine, the hips will move back into the right spot.

With lordosis the head is just a little bit too far back—it's not centered on the top of the spine. Here the hips move back a little and that puts a lot of strain on the lower back so the bottom part of the back begins to arch too much. So again, by moving the head—in this case, just a little bit further forward—and centering it atop your spine, the muscles in the body will be allowed to relax.

NeuroCranial Restructuring

You may notice when you look into the mirror that:

- your eyes are not level and your head might be tilted to one side

- one shoulder may be obviously higher than the other

- one ear could be closer to one shoulder, or
- your eyes and ears might be out of alignment.

These are all indications of subtle structural imbalances that can affect your entire body.

The best treatment I've discovered for scoliosis, kyphosis, and lordosis was developed by Dr. Dean Howell. The technique is called NeuroCranial Restructuring (often called NCR). Dr. Howell specializes in realigning the bones of the skull and aligning the skull on top of the spine. Absolutely nothing else comes close to what NCR can do for you, in my opinion. You could be going to chiropractors for the rest of your life to loosen up tightness in your spine, but in most cases, you will not be treating the cause of the problem.

You may have already addressed the issues related to your feet and hips and you may no longer have pain issues after doing that, especially if you have addressed the chemistry issues to help deal with the pain. However, if your head is out of alignment, that is still going to put strain on your neck, shoulders, and back, which will translate all the way down through your system.

NCR is a series of four treatments over four days, costing a total of about $1,000. For extreme cases of kyphosis, lordosis, and scoliosis, you might want to consider this top-down approach, especially if you have not received sufficient benefit from working with your feet and hips from the bottom up.

One of the good things about NCR is that it not only puts your head on straight and corrects neck and back pain issues, but it also improves facial alignment and facial structure. Most people know that facial symmetry adds to beauty, however that is only one of five components. Someone considered to be a beautiful person will usually have:

- a symmetrical, oval-shaped face
- a broad forehead
- high cheekbones, and
- "large" eyes (let me elaborate... large eyes could look odd, what I mean by this term is wide-open, innocent-appearing eyes—often called "doe-eyes").

It is very common, especially for people who were born with the use of forceps, for there to be compression in and around the temple area of the head. With a lot of people, their eyes are not as open as they could be or one eye is more open than the other. Similarly, one ear may be lower than the other. Cheekbones may also be sunken, which alters the dimension of the face. In addition, the forehead may not be as broad as it could be.

NCR is wonderful if you are considering making an

improvement to your appearance. Plastic surgery is much more expensive, and in my opinion, the best way to improve the beauty of your face is to improve the natural alignment of the bones in your head, which NCR can achieve very well.

If you have ever considered a nose job or similar facial surgery to improve your appearance, then you might also consider NCR as it will help with your appearance and your structure. It will also help to improve your mental and emotional self because the bones in your head become more ideal and improve the flow of cerebrospinal fluid within your brain. In addition, the bone which you are adjusting through NCR is right above the hypothalamus, which is your main hormonal emotional center.

NCR also routinely improves ear, nose, and throat conditions, reducing snoring, eliminating ear and sinus drainage issues, and can even benefit one's hearing. Also, migraine headache suffers who believe they have "tried everything" routinely benefit from as little as one series of NCR treatments.

You are optimizing all of these things with one great treatment, and I can't say enough great things about NCR—there is absolutely nothing that comes even close to being as good, in my opinion.

While NCR is a great treatment, it is not yet available in every location. If it is unavailable where you live, then you might consider some alternatives.

One alternative you could look at to balance the body from the top down is called Atlas Profilax (atlasprofilax.com). If neither NCR nor Atlas Profilax is available, then you may want to consider osteopathy or Rolfing.

Posture Makes Perfect

The end result we're seeking through addressing our structural alignment is optimal posture.

When the body is maintained in a position of optimal posture, chronic pains disappear. However, even if a person were to have near perfect structural alignment, postural habits need to be addressed to ensure pain-free living for years to come. The Alexander Technique is worth studying if you would like to stand tall and live pain-free into your golden years.

If you're not keen to study Alexander Technique, here is some common sense I've learned when it comes to posture:

- Stand tall with your head above your spine as though it were suspended on a string held from above.

- When sitting, avoid slouching. Try to keep your feet flat on the floor and your upper body upright with your shoulders open (back). In today's computer age, many of us have our shoulders rolled forward as we type on our keyboards, so consider getting an ergonomic keyboard. Also, make sure you get up and move around every 60-90 minutes.

- When lying in bed, it's best to lie on your back. Lying on the stomach is the worst as it encourages lordosis (swayback) and stretches the neck to one side. Lying on your side encourages scoliosis by rolling your bottom shoulder inward and rotating your hips out of alignment.

  Lying on your back with a contour pillow supporting your neck, and your legs parallel, is ideal. If your legs make more of a figure four arrangement, this encourages your hips to be out of alignment. To train yourself to keep your legs parallel, you could consider wearing a loose-fitting belt around both your thighs for a few weeks or place a couple of pillows under your knees. This latter suggestion also removes strain from your lower back if this is a reason you prefer not to sleep on your back.

Energetic Pain

Acupuncture is being increasingly accepted by conventional medicine. There is good reason for this: for many people, acupuncture can demonstrate incredible results for dealing with pain.

There are other treatments for energetic pain; take headaches as an example. One of the most effective techniques for headaches is EFT (Emotional Freedom Techniques®) which are discussed in greater detail in chapter 2. Reiki is another option for relieving the body of pain.

The homeopathic remedy Traumeel, which was introduced earlier in this chapter, is another excellent example of the effectiveness of energetic medicine for pain. Homeopathic medicine is another branch in the advanced field of energy medicine.

Louise Hay (who I mentioned earlier in the book) has determined that energetic pains can be directly correlated to feelings of guilt. This is not as strange as it may seem—when we feel guilty about something, we subconsciously believe that we should suffer. If your pain is attributable to guilt, then an immediate way to address pain is to identify—and then treat—the underlying guilt.

Life Without Pain

So there you have it.

We started from the feet because that treatment is the least expensive and also achieves the quickest results. For just $100, you can have three sets of the Barefoot Science foot strengthening system and your natural arch will return. Your ankles will improve their strength and alignment, and your knees will start feeling better, which is going to take strain off of your hips and lower back.

Then, you will want to start strengthening and loosening up the core of your body and keeping that loose. If you like hula hooping, consider doing that again. As well as addressing structural pain, you also need to look at addressing energetic pain.

Finally, if you still have neck and back pain, or if you have some facial features that you would like improved, then I recommend you look at NCR.

Chapter 8
Terminally Well

There are many examples of terminal illnesses which provide rich fodder for the tabloid media and television dramas.

When I hear the term terminal disease, I like to think of two categories:

- Illnesses we are told will drastically shorten our life expectancy so that it can be measured in months rather than years.

- Illnesses that may not have a significant effect on our life expectancy, but which we are told are incurable or will be with us until we die.

I want to look at both of these types of terminal disease. However, rather than thinking in terms of illness, let's focus on wellness. So far in this book we have looked at addressing non-fatal illnesses and life-enhancing treatments. If you have been following these ideas so far, then you will probably be enjoying a healthy life, so in this chapter I want to look at possible treatments you could consider if you contract a terminal condition or if a family member or friend contracts such a condition.

My intention here is not to suggest that these are sure-fire, guaranteed cures, but instead to point you at a range of treatments that could be highly effective. I believe in all these treatments. I am not asking you to believe in them, but instead, I am asking you to think about them and to conduct your own due diligence. In this way, you will be better informed if you or a family member or friend is ever in a position where they could benefit from one of these treatments. Not only will you be better informed and have acquired some background knowledge in a non-stressful environment, but you will have choices, meaning you can find the treatment that is right for you (or your friend/family member).

Immediate Life-Threatening Conditions

Let's start by looking at the immediate life threatening conditions—you know the obvious candidates: cancer and AIDS. With the later stages of these conditions, life expectancy can often be defined in terms of months and can be considerably less than a year. These are the most dreaded diseases, often described as being someone's worst nightmare.

When someone is diagnosed with a terminal, life-threatening disease, then this is the time to fast-track the healing process. A terminal disease also provides much greater motivation to try things one might not normally try, treatments which might be more drastic, and protocols which may lead to more dramatic lifestyle changes. Let me offer some ideas.

EBOO

In chapter 3 I talk about EBOO (Extracorporeal Blood Oxygenation and Ozonation) but I think it is worth mentioning again. EBOO is a blood filtration process which is combined with the introduction of high doses of ozone.

If I ever become terminally ill with AIDS or Hepatitis C, I will do whatever possible to receive a series of EBOO treatments and I will take this treatment in conjunction with intravenous nutrients.

Fasting and Juice Fasting

In their natural environment wild animals don't eat when they are sick, so why do we?

Food nourishes our bodies, but can also nourish disease. However, unlike our bodies, disease dies far more swiftly when it is not provided with nutrition. Therefore one of the first procedures to consider when diagnosed with a life-threatening condition is fasting. This may be total fasting (in other words, taking no food and only water) or juice fasting (in other words, only consuming fruit and vegetable juice which you have prepared yourself from fresh fruit and vegetables).

Clearly, this type of regime is quite a significant change. If you are living a poor lifestyle (perhaps eating lots of fried food and drinking a lot of alcohol) this might be a significant dietary change. However, this sort of dramatic change may be necessary if you're living with a life sentence.

Master Cleanse

I've already mentioned the book *The Master Cleanser* by Stanley Burroughs (and you can find details at CraigBrockie.com/Reading) which describes the Master Cleanse. The Master Cleanse is called by many different names—for instance, you may have heard it referred to as the Lemon Cleanse or the Lemonade Diet. If you want to know the process to follow, then I suggest you check out the book.

If you are seriously ill—especially if you have a terminal condition—then the Master Cleanse offers a huge range of benefits:

- The Internal Body Wash (also known as the salt water flush) is a daily part of the routine, fast-tracking colon and liver health.

- Fresh lemon juice and maple syrup combine to

provide an excellent natural source of vitamins, minerals and enzymes, all key components for healing.

- Replacing solid with liquid food allows the body to maintain a high-energy state and focus more resources on healing and less on digestion.

If you're sick, then by following the Master Cleanse you will be taking a burden off your digestive system as it will not have to process solid food. This will also take a burden off the body so it can focus on the job at hand: eliminating the illness.

By consuming a liquid that is loaded with nutrition and enzymes, you will be helping the body to sustain itself and to heal. Burroughs also recommends rinsing out the intestines and colon every day, helping to further eliminate toxins from the body.

In my opinion, if you're looking for a well-balanced, affordable process for addressing illness, this is it!! Burroughs first published his book in 1941, so this cannot be regarded as a new and untested option.

Even if you don't have a terminal illness, you can still undertake a Master Cleanse. One benefit that many people find is that it encourages excess weight loss.

Gerson Protocol

The Gerson Protocol emphasizes juicing. Where the Master Cleanse is applicable in many situations, one of which may be cancer, the Gerson Protocol is intended specifically for curing cancer.

The Protocol has been established for decades and there is a large body of evidence to support the benefits of the Protocol in curing cancers. The Protocol has up to an 80% success rate in treating some terminal cancers. As well as providing evidence for the Gerson Protocol, this research demonstrates that non-conventional therapies can have a positive impact, even if the mainstream medical system has yet to adopt the practices.

Many of us—perhaps most, if not all of us—have met someone who is undergoing conventional treatment for cancer. These patients will be loaded with drugs and then have chemotherapy or radiation therapy for weeks or months. Many times, the treatment feels worse than the illness, with the immune system getting shot to pieces, hair falling out, and so on. Not only can the treatment be terrifying for the patient, but often the situation for family and friends is dire, since they are unable to aid the patient. So it is good to know that there are treatment options, such as the Gerson Protocol, which are not so detrimental to one's quality of life.

The Gerson Protocol is also featured in some detail

in the movie *The Beautiful Truth* (which was also mentioned it the last chapter).

Dr. Hulda Clark's 21-Day Cancer Elimination Program

In many ways Dr. Hulda Clark is one of the most controversial people in the alternative health scene. However, if you achieve the same level of results that she does, and if you start showing that more expensive treatments are less effective, then you're going to ruffle some feathers.

If I were diagnosed with terminal cancer, I would immediately begin Dr. Clark's 21-day Cancer Cure which boasts a success rate of 95% with advanced cancers (stage four and five cancers, including those with a prognosis of imminent death). Before her retirement, Clark was willing to accept any patient for treatment—irrespective of their condition—and her success rate was as close to a guaranteed cure as you will find.

Clark recommends a package of supplements which covers the complete protocol. Within a few days, malignant tumors become benign, and after 21 days, you are cured.

Royal Raymond Rife was an inventor who was well-documented in the 1930s to be curing cancer with specific energetic frequencies. Rife found that, in the same way that an opera singer can destroy a wine glass by singing at the glass's resonant frequency, cancers could be destroyed by vibrating the cancer at its resonant frequency.

Dr. Clark has taken Rife's work and further developed it. In addition to her frequency generator-based treatment (she calls it zapping) Dr. Clark also emphasizes vitamins and nutrients in her supplements as well as action to remove toxins. Rife only looked at frequencies—he did not consider nutrition or toxins.

Dr. Clark uses a device called a synchrometer to scan the body. From these results she can determine which particular toxin, parasite, or virus is affecting the patient's body. This energy-based testing is similar to the process used for allergy testing. The assessment process seeks to find whether the patient resonates with a specific frequency. Similar assessment technologies are the Vega Test, MORA therapy, and Orion BodyScan devices.

Go to CraigBrockie.com/Clark to find out more about Dr. Clark and her work.

Life-Long Conditions

Then there are other diseases that are life-long conditions. These illnesses will not kill you immediately, but they are terminal conditions in that—according to conventional beliefs—once you have these illnesses, you have them until you die. Typical examples of these diseases include diabetes and bipolar disorder.

My Dad's Story

Let me tell you a bit about my dad.

He had been a long-term sufferer of bipolar disorder and as a result had been on psychiatric medications for over 40 years. Side effects from his medications caused him to develop a tremor, memory loss, and eventually symptoms of Parkinson's disease. Although he was on anti-anxiety medication, he was one of the most anxious people I've ever known, so obviously the drug wasn't even doing what it was prescribed to do.

My dad undertook a medically-supervised detoxification program involving intravenous nutrient therapy. The doctors succeeded in getting him (prescription) drug free so that he could begin the Hubbard Sauna Protocol (which is mentioned it chapter 6). When he stopped taking his medications his tremor disappeared, and by the end of his sauna program all Parkinson's symptoms were gone and his memory had improved.

Most conventional detox centers specialize in replacing street drug and alcohol addictions with addictions to prescription psych medications. The end result is that the patient is still addicted to mood-altering drugs with dangerous side effects.

It's ironic these institutions call themselves detox centers because they usually have nothing to do with detoxifying their patients. We've discussed detoxification in great detail in this book, so you can appreciate how replacing one drug addiction with another has nothing to do with detoxification.

There are very few holistic detox centers that specialize in helping people withdraw from prescription medications such as antidepressants or anti-anxiety medications and then purifying their bodies. Fortunately, there are many more holistic detox centers that help alcohol and street drug users get clean and purify their bodies. Although the Purification Program is available as an introductory service through every Church of Scientology, unfortunately they do not accept anyone until they are psychotropic substance-free (both street drug and prescription medication free). If you or a loved one want to gain freedom from drugs or alcohol, visit CraigBrockie.com/Well for related resources.

Diabetes

Some people are told that they have diabetes.

On hearing the news, the patient assumes this is a life sentence and that all they can do is to take an appropriate amount of insulin to keep their blood sugar levels in check. However, Dr. Gabriel Cousens M.D. is featured in an excellent documentary where, through a radical change in diet, he reversed diabetes in a group of individuals in less than a month.

You can find the links to his videos from my website. Go to CraigBrockie.com/Videos to see more.

Obesity

A lot of people think that obesity is a life-long condition. It's not!!

I hope that in reading through this book and trying some of the ideas, you will have found yourself at a weight that you are happy with. However, if you're not, then you could check out *The Weight Loss Cure "They" Don't Want You to Know About* by Kevin Trudeau (Alliance Publishing Group, 2008) which reintroduces the concept of HCG. HCG resets the hypothalamus gland and thereby resets the metabolism. The program lasts about four weeks and one can expect to lose a significant amount of weight in that time.

Are Any Diseases Truly Incurable?

Bipolar disorder, diabetes, and obesity are just three examples of many diseases that have been widely diagnosed to patients as incurable or genetic. Perhaps you have been diagnosed with multiple sclerosis, fibromyalgia, or HIV. Maybe you've been diagnosed with clinical depression or one of the many anxiety disorders and given medication to take for the rest of your life.

It really doesn't matter which disease or disorder

you have been diagnosed with, you have a choice. You have the choice of either believing your condition is incurable or not. If you choose the latter and take control of your health, you have an excellent opportunity to break free from the symptoms of the disease and master the art of wellness. I sincerely hope you choose this option.

Becoming Terminally Well

As I said at the top of this chapter, my aim in this section of the book is not to offer specific answers to specific health issues. Instead, I have offered a range of ideas that you can evaluate and share with your family and friends. You may not want to use these treatments in your everyday life, however, if you have a terminal illness, you'll be glad you did the research.

Chapter 9
Pay it Forward: Mastering the Art of Wellness

I hope you have found this book both interesting and entertaining, but more importantly, I hope you have felt a positive improvement in your health.

Whatever change you have found, this is only the start of your journey to life-long health and happiness. As part of this journey, it is important that you:

- remember what you have learned, and
- deepen your understanding of health-related issues.

Luckily, there is a way to do both!! And it's simple

to do both at the same time: talk about what you have found.

Take a moment or two to reach out to someone who needs your help—someone who will benefit from learning about some of the ideas that you have found in this book, someone whose life could be radically transformed by them taking control of their health. You don't need to force these ideas on them—in a calm and non-judgmental way you can explain what you have learned and share your first-hand experiences.

All you have to do is tell the truth. By teaching what you have learned you will gain a deeper understanding of the principles in this book and you will also motivate yourself to improve your health even further. Also, by trying to look at a health issue from someone else's perspective, you may inadvertently uncover a health challenge you had not realized that you needed to address.

By sharing what you have learned, you will also become part of the solution, and part of a wider movement of people who are dedicated to working together to improve their own health, their family's health, and their friends' health. If you're looking for something unique and easy to share, then tell your family and friends about FreeShield.com so they can start taking action to minimize electromagnetic stress.

If you want to tell people about this book, there is a free extract available on my website (go to CraigBrockie.com/TakeControl to get this). This extract includes the introduction to the book and the first chapter, plus the table of contents, which explains what the book is about. You can send this extract to as many of your friends as you like.

I would also encourage you to join and interact with the community. Join us at Forums.CraigBrockie.com where you can read about the latest developments and share experiences with other people who are trying to improve their health. You can also join us on the third Saturday of every month for our regular liver flush.

So this is your call to action—go and spread the word!!

Take Control of Your Health

Epilogue

I would like to add a few personal thoughts around the health care debate (that's the wider debate about how we all achieve wellness, not the debate over health insurance coverage that is presently being fought in the United States).

Conventional Wisdom?

The term "conventional wisdom" has been proven time and time again to be a combination of two words that truly do not belong together. Conventional wisdom is simply popular opinion, which is just that, opinion, and it's often wrong.

Many of those who introduce novel ideas like drawing attention to historic examples of popular opinion being way off the mark. For instance:

- For many years the earth was believed to be flat.

- In the early 1970s the phenomenon of global cooling was identified. This had a scientific basis—global temperatures between the 1940s and the 1970s did fall. However, this data was extrapolated with the result that conventional wisdom accepted that the world was entering a new ice age. Almost no one takes that view today!

- Galileo spent decades trying to convince people that gravitational pull applied equally to light objects as it did to heavy objects.

When it comes to health, we can find many recent examples of conventional folly. For instance, if we take a moment to think about it, we can recall the continuous flip-flopping of diet trends. At one time many "experts" had us believe our main adversary was the almighty calorie. A few years later, fat became our fiercely feared foe. Then the "war on carbs" began and protein was awarded hero status. I've tuned out most of this nonsense the past few years, but notice that trans-fats now seem to be the evil villain.

The Truth

It is said that all truth passes through three stages. First, it is ridiculed. Second, it is violently opposed. Third, it is accepted as self-evident.

Although I advocate in this book that you take

control of your health, I would remind you to consult accredited healthcare practitioners to assist you with your journey. You are also encouraged to do your own due diligence about things I suggest rather than jump into them blindly.

As you research the ideas I have introduced in this book—particularly if you carry out your research on the internet, you are likely to come across people discrediting the same ideas that I've found to be effective. These sources often appear to be credible and well intentioned. However, critics are seldom either.

Whether supported by vested interests or simply fueled by ignorance and arrogance, you'll find that critics of the safe, affordable, and effective concepts I've shared with you like to use fear tactics to scare you away from them.

You will also notice that seldom, if ever, have critics tried the idea themselves. Instead they prefer to tell you why, in their opinion, an idea won't work or why they think it might be dangerous. It's really quite ridiculous. A good example relates to a popular video I have on YouTube that teaches people how to safely dilute food grade hydrogen peroxide and use it for dental hygiene. I regularly have people say that what I'm doing is dangerous, yet I've been using hydrogen peroxide when I brush and floss my teeth daily for several years and know firsthand how safe it is.

Even my dentist, the same man who was astounded by the excellent condition of my dental health when I walked in his clinic, said that hydrogen peroxide was bad for my teeth according to his association. Again, not because he had tried it himself—after all, who would want to do something that could be dangerous?

Now, let's ask ourselves a question. Does the dental industry benefit from people coming in for regular dental cleanings and repairs, or by their patients being perfectly fine without them? This is a simple conflict of interest and remember, it's no big conspiracy, it's just business. Realize that this applies not only to dentistry, but the entire health care system. Profits come before people and unfortunately, it's far more profitable to maintain disease than it is to prevent or cure disease.

While these multi-billion dollar industries are unlikely to begin putting ethics ahead of profits, fortunately there are MDs who understand the merits of holistic medicine and have begun to use it as an addition to their conventional practices.

Positive Signs of Truth

When a holistic health truth starts challenging the status quo, first it is ridiculed and its promoters are discredited. As ironic as it sounds, being featured on critical health-related websites usually indicates success in the holistic health field. It means that the truth has helped enough people and gained enough attention that those with conflicting interests felt it was necessary to discredit it.

If a holistic doctor is really "lucky," the FDA or state department comes in and pulls their license or drags them into court for some frivolous reason. These actions, even if they are successfully defended, are used as further evidence of the doctor being of questionable character, or their treatment being hazardous. Meanwhile, thousands of people are being killed by prescription drugs and it's business as usual.

Thankfully, there are also excellent web sites like curezone.com and television programs like Oprah that bravely take a genuine interest in the well being of their audiences by sharing the truth about holistic medicine—its benefits, success stories, and the scientific research backing it up.

As we take control of our health and master the art of wellness, our physical, mental, and emotional capacities increase, and we develop the required resources and critical thinking skills to allow us to achieve where others fail. Let's remember to use the force wisely by using our increased personal power to help others get a leg up. Our world is certainly in need of positive role models and leaders of high integrity.

Scientific Proof and Double-Blind Studies

Another popular way to discredit holistic health truths is to say that there's no science that proves them to be effective. And if a double-blind study has never been conducted, well then it must be quackery.

In most cases, plenty of scientific research and clinical trials do support holistic health treatments, but this data is dismissed. In some cases, sufficient scientific data may not exist, but only due to lack of funding to conduct the research. I'd love to see the various disease societies, associations, and foundations fund this research.

Yet, conventional medicine is less scientific than we've been led to believe. For instance, in the multibillion dollar psychiatric drug industry, the message is about one's brain chemistry being out of balance and the effectiveness of using drugs to restore the desired equilibrium.

Well, guess what, there is no scientific test used in modern psychiatry to determine one's brain chemistry. Psychiatrists use absolute subjectivity to determine what a patient's brain chemistry imbalance *might* be and write a prescription based on their best guess. Ironically, it is the holistic medical field that now has a laboratory test to measure neurotransmitter levels.

The film *Psychiatry: An Industry of Death* (cchr.org) is perhaps the most disturbing documentary I have ever seen. Seeing the torture psychiatric patients have been subjected to throughout history and hearing the countless stories of parents whose children have committed suicide soon after being prescribed antidepressant drugs is alarming. Although psychiatrists genuinely want to help their patients, the tools they have at their disposal are limited.

The affordable health alternatives introduced in *Take Control of Your Health* have years of clinical trials, and in many cases, double-blind studies backing up their safety and effectiveness, and instead of making you want to end your life, you'll begin feeling so good people will notice and start asking you what your secret is.

Take Control of Your Wealth

Conventional wisdom spreads far beyond medicine and into every walk of life.

A good friend of mine and one of the brightest and most logical people I've ever met is a gentleman named Steven Jon Kaplan. Steve writes a daily investment newsletter (TrueContrarian.com) and has accurately identified the mainstream media as the one of the best counter-indicators there is.

A counter-indicator is an indicator that shows the opposite of what you are trying to prove.

What this means is that by the time the non-financial media are most strongly promoting an idea, then there is a benefit to taking the opposite course. For instance, if the media are saying the price of something can only go higher, this is a strong indicator to sell.

I will look at many of these ideas and challenge many widely held conventional beliefs in my next book, *Take Control of Your Wealth*. Check out CraigBrockie.com/Wealth for further details.

Where Credit Is Due…

This is the first edition of my first book—I will continually improve this book and will supplement the information it contains with further materials on my website. In addition, from time to time I will release a new edition of this book with the latest improvements.

I've purposely provided information in a concise form to avoid this book being an overly technical, intimidating read. The idea is for you to take control of your health and in order for you to do so you really need to become an eager and discerning student. On a related note, it is often said that there is no such thing as an original idea. At the very least, original ideas appear to be quite rare. While I've done my best to credit whomever I learned a particular idea from, there remain two challenges:

1) I've learned everything I know from other people and do not recall where every idea has come from.

2) The people I've learned from are likely not the first people to think of the ideas either. That said, if you feel someone in particular is deserving of credit in this book, I appreciate you sharing that with me via CraigBrockie.com/Improvements and I will make sure I acknowledge the right people.

Also, on a related note, I realize I have as much, or more, to learn from you as you do from me. I therefore appreciate you sharing your success stories and any suggestions for improving this book with me.

Freedom of Choice

In closing, on a more serious note, your support is very important to maintain our freedom of choice in connection with our healthcare. If you have implemented some of the ideas presented in this book, you will know firsthand that holistic health care solutions are far more than the quackery that they are made out to be by those with conflicting interests.

Please take a few moments to research the topic of Codex Alementarus. Essentially, the current chemical, food, and medical interests are intent on eliminating many of our current health freedoms. For instance, one of the proposed changes if Codex is implemented is that all foods be irradiated. Irradiation of food destroys all of the enzymes. Enzymes are important, remember?

Another proposed legislation if Codex is adopted is that we would require a doctor's prescription in order to buy basic natural supplements such as vitamin C. Not only would dispensing fees and the cost of supplements increase the price, but the likelihood of doctors prescribing dosages beyond the RDA is doubtful. I much prefer being the one to decide what natural supplements I consume and pay a fair price for buying them.

The good news is that you can make a difference. Already in Canada, two votes to implement Codex legislation have failed to pass due to the response from concerned citizens.

Now that you have taken control of your health, you know the truth: there are viable solutions outside of the mainstream drugs-and-surgery paradigm.

Thank you for playing an active role in maintaining our freedom of choice, and our health.

Further Resources

I hope you have enjoyed the book.

The benefits don't end here. Come over to CraigBrockie.com/TakeControl where you will find many further resources to help you optimize and maintain your health. Among other things, you will find:

- My recommended further reading list.

- My recommended viewing list.

- Details of some of the leading practitioners in the holistic medicine field.

- My recommendations for supplements and products I use and where you can get these.

- My dietary recommendations.

And you can also sign up for my regular newsletter,

which looks at health and related issues.

In addition, you can join our forums and talk to other people who are interested in optimizing their health. You can find the forums at Forums.CraigBrockie.com.

I'm also available for one-on-one telephone consultations and public speaking engagements. Refer to my web site for details.

I look forward to keeping in touch with you.

Be well,

Craig